WE

The Antidote to Divorce

PATRICK IGBINIJESU

ISBN 979-8-88616-481-7 (paperback)
ISBN 979-8-88616-482-4 (digital)

Copyright © 2022 by Patrick Igbinijesu

All rights reserved. No part of this publication may be reproduced, distributed, or transmitted in any form or by any means, including photocopying, recording, or other electronic or mechanical methods without the prior written permission of the publisher. For permission requests, solicit the publisher via the address below.

Christian Faith Publishing
832 Park Avenue
Meadville, PA 16335
www.christianfaithpublishing.com

All scripture quotations are from the New King James Version (NKJV) of the Bible, unless otherwise stated.

Printed in the United States of America

Chapter 1

The State of Our Marriages

I have a passion for marriage.

But I have an even deeper passion for the way that marriage is the apt depiction of our walk with the Lord Jesus Christ.

When I refer to our walk with the Lord Jesus Christ, I make an assumption that you have been born again and filled with the Holy Spirit with the evidence of speaking in tongues. If you haven't, please do not be deterred. The intention of this book is to communicate how vital the gospel of Christ is to your marriage.

I see clearly the global need for the gospel, particularly as it pertains to marriage because the very essence of Jesus's death, burial, and resurrection was to contract a marriage between God and all of humanity. And therein, the conjoining of God and man lies an opening which, if explored, could transform our homes and marriages into havens of bliss.

The only pertinent question is this: will we be able to enter through these doors, flung open, for our entrance? The state of our marriages is an all-important factor in the enshrining of healthy families and communities.

In fact, I have recently found new meaning in the words *the state of our marriages*.

Everything in society depends on the way things are on the home front. It all depends on the readiness and willingness of a husband and his wife to yield to the wisdom of God; without this, the structure of society collapses. It is not the state of our homes—that the place be peaceful and free of conflict—that will matter much but the state of our marriages. It will influence the kind of men and women we become, the kind of children we raise, and the quality of decisions we make, be it about personal finance or climate change.

It is worthwhile to ponder what some concerned-thought leaders have said about the quality of today's marriages.

As we examine our marriages to determine which of the states they are in, it is imperative to note that marriage originated in God. It is also imperative to understand that, without God at the center of our marriages, we are prone to struggle and unhappiness. Also, without a map or a tour guide, we, who are married—or want to be married—are in over our heads, lost in uncharted territory fraught with the land mines that lead to doubt, frustration, infidelity, and, ultimately, divorce.

The other thing to understand is that the gospel is both our map and tour guide; two blessings in one, which show us that divorce was clearly not God's plan for marriage. Jesus said, "From the beginning, it was not so" (Matthew 19:8). And He could say this of divorce with flawless accuracy because He was there with God in the beginning, "and without Him nothing was made that was made" (John 1:1–3). Not even marriage was made without the consortium of God and His Word.

All through the Bible, we see the tapestry of a conjoining, from God and His Word to Adam and Eve and all the way to Christ and His church. It is what the state of every marriage should be, although this is far from reality.

Today, the pundits generally say that one in two marriages will end in divorce. Even though the very substance of this statistic seems highly contestable, the general import of it is that the understanding of what a marriage is, is lacking.

Thoughts About Divorce

A few years ago, Hollywood actor Gwyneth Paltrow popularized the phrase *conscious uncoupling* to mean "the act of ending a marriage amicably in such a way that the former spouses remain friends, continue to co-parent if they have children, and, possibly, stay in love."

I don't know whether it was the idea of being in love without monogamous commitment or the offer of a smooth transition back to singleness that won widespread appeal among so many, but a divorce—no matter how amicable—is not without its attendant pain points.

Uncoupling—whether it be conscious or not—is always gut-wrenching in some way, for at least one of the spouses, because it is unnatural if you go by those words of Jesus: "From the beginning it was not so."

Simply put, the rampant divorce problem across the world today is not primarily one of irreconcilable differences as divorce lawsuits often indicate. The real issue is a lack of understanding of the states our marriages are in and how to change a marriage from one state to another.

For a Christian, the state your marriage is in is a direct reflection of the state of your Christianity. Paul, the apostle, called it "a great mystery" (Ephesians 5:31–32), which I will deal with later on.

Until you understand the state of your marriage, there will always be pain, whether you choose to stay married or get a divorce. The secret doorway back to a healthy, thriving marriage is to focus on the state your marriage is in now and not to do away with the marriage itself.

Divorcing your spouse and remarrying someone else will not resolve the pain. In fact, studies have shown that the likelihood of people, who had previously undergone a divorce, getting another divorce increased with each successive marriage.

And He [Jesus] answered and said to them,
"Have you not read that He who made them at
the beginning 'made them male and female,' and

said, 'For this reason a man shall leave his father and mother and be joined to his wife, and the two shall become one flesh'? So then, they are no longer two but one flesh. Therefore what God has joined together, let not man separate." (Matthew 19:4–6)

No matter where you are in your marriage, God's idea is never for it to end in divorce. His idea is for it to end with the death of one or both spouses. It is also not His will for anyone—including you—to end your marriage, even under dire circumstances. Nothing could be more displeasing to God than to put an end to something He initiated, no matter how you got married.

Look at it this way: being in a marriage is like being part of a set of conjoined twins, sharing the same vital organs. Separating them could lead to the demise of both.

I recently came across the story of Chang and Eng Bunker, a set of conjoined twins from whose birthplace the term *Siamese twins* originated.

Born in Siam (now Thailand) in the early nineteenth century to poor parents, the twin brothers—joined at the sternum with their livers fused together, even though the organs were independent of each other—somehow wound up rich, celebrity, married to two sisters, fathering twenty-one children between them.

Despite the oddity of their physical condition, the Bunker brothers managed to lead very productive lives, albeit not without hitches. They lost most of their money during the American Civil War, and even though they coped well, Chang suffered a stroke and partial paralysis; after which, he began drinking heavily. He remained in poor health, and on January 17, 1874, he passed away in his sleep. When Eng woke up to find his brother deceased, he cried, "Then, I am going!"

I imagine that the Bunker brothers had a profound acceptance of each other that every married couple should have: though flawed to the outside world, those two shared an undeniable bond that could only have been dissolved in death.

Marriage is this way too. When we marry someone, we are conjoined to that person till death. Otherwise, why are husbands told "to love their wives as their own bodies"? Or that "he that loves his wife loves himself"?

The presupposition here trails back to Adam in the Garden of Eden, when he first saw Eve and said, "This is now bone of my bones, and flesh of my flesh: she shall be called Woman, because she was taken out of Man" (Genesis 2:23).

Three Important Things on Marriage

Having researched the subject of marriage for many years, my conclusions are as follows:

- Marriage requires knowledge.
- Marriage has different seasons.
- Marriage is always in a particular state.

Marriage requires knowledge.

The biggest challenge to marriages across the world is knowledge. God declared it back in the Old Testament that: without knowledge, people perish (Hosea 4:6). And I might add that: without knowledge, a marriage perishes.

Since a marriage is the fashioning of a new person—from two people—by God, it is only right to approach your spouse not as a partner but as a part of you yet to be discovered.

"*And they two shall be one flesh: so then they are no more two, but one flesh*" (Mark 10:8).

Do you understand the import of being one with this person you are married to? The general misunderstanding of this oneness that is marriage is what has wrecked many homes. Knowing your spouse should be a lifelong commitment once you accept him or her as a part of you. "*Likewise, ye husbands, dwell with them according to knowledge, giving honour unto the wife, as unto the weaker vessel, and as being heirs together of the grace of life; that your prayers be not hindered*" (1 Peter 3:7).

In essence, a husband is to dwell with his wife based on knowledge, valuing her not as his partner but as a delicate part of himself, and vice versa. The word translated *knowledge* is the Greek word *gnosis* from which we derive English words like *diagnosis* or *prognosis*. The idea these words communicate is progressive knowledge—that marriage should be a lifelong commitment to study the person we marry while making ourselves open enough to be studied by them as well.

Marriage has different seasons.

Typically, marriage happens in phases. For most marriages, the lovers are lured into saying, "I do," basking in the passion, the romance, and the thrill of being around each other. It is the phase where you and your spouse are like peas in a pod. In this season, everything about your relationship is full of promise—the joy of children, thriving careers, a beautiful home, and, most of all, the assurance of someone to share it with. I call this the *Oxytocin Phase*.

But then, that season is quickly overtaken by a season of realization when the rubber finally meets the road. In this season, couples begin to see each other for who they really are. The fog of fantasy clears, leaving the stark facts about this person you married in full view. This is the *Settling-down Phase*. The unsettling aspect of this phase could be the manner in which you respond to the new discoveries you are making about your spouse. Seeds of conflict are sown in this phase that begin to escalate in the next phase.

The next phase is the *Critical Phase*. It is usually characterized by intense conflict based on your preformed expectations and the need to try to manage those expectations, and a power struggle ensues as the couple tries to establish a kind of order, a way things should be in the marriage. Quite often, one spouse will push to dominate while the other spouse will push back, leading to an escalation of conflict. This phase is where marriages are most predisposed to all kinds of infidelity and, ultimately, divorce. This phase is one of the reasons why I wrote this book: to help you navigate through this season of your marriage. If you hang in there, making the decision to know your spouse better, understand the season you are in, and alter the state of your marriage, you can make it through to the next phase.

The next season is typically cathartic. The spouses, having weathered the power struggle born out of being different individuals, learn to accept, forgive, and cooperate with each other. This is where the real cleaving happens in a marriage, where maturity sets in. Most marriages that fail never get into the *Maturity Phase* for the lack of knowledge.

You need to know what a marriage is. And no one can define it better than its creator—God. You need to know the season your marriage is in. While the passing of time will take you from the Oxytocin Phase through the Settling-down and Critical Phases of your marriage, only knowing the season you are in and what state your marriage is in can take your union to maturity.

Marriage is always in a particular state.

As I wrote earlier, understanding the state your marriage is in is more important than understanding marriage itself. Why do people get divorced and tear down their whole lives when they could have simply tweaked the state of their marriage?

If you have contemplated divorce, know this: even if you marry someone else and are happy at the beginning, you will still need to learn how to shift your marriage from one state to another over the different seasons. The stats show that divorced people are two times more likely to get divorced again than couples who are in their first marriage. There is a godly way to tweak the state of a marriage.

First, what do I mean when I say, "The state of a marriage"?

By state, I mean the type of relationship you presently have with your spouse (which is often a reflection of the type you presently have with the Lord Jesus Christ). Every marriage is always in one of three states: a state of codependency, a state of partnership, or a state of union. And while I will deal with these states in later chapters, what guarantees the success of your marriage is knowing God's original plan for marriage, discerning the season or phase your marriage is in, and understanding the state of your marriage.

In his book, *Getting Married*, George Bernard Shaw noted:

> When two people are under the influence of the most violent, most insane, most delusive, and most transient of passions, they are required to swear that they will remain in that excited, abnormal, and exhausting condition continuously until death do them part.

Shaw rightly accepts the transitory nature of the seasons and conditions of marriage. However, this book seeks to help couples manage the transient using the immutable.

Chapter 2

Is Marriage an Outdated Tradition?

An article appeared in the *Huffington Post* titled "Is Marriage an Outdated Tradition?" The author of the article began by alluding to marriage as an illusion we have been socialized from childhood to accept—finding that special person to spend the rest of your life with.

He said, "We are under the illusion that marriage is something that means we're going to spend the rest of our lives with somebody. But that is just an illusion."

In the course of his remarks, he expressed a fundamental misconception that "marriage has become antiquated in the sense that we need to stay until death do us part," advocating a surrender to the notion of having five to six loving adult relationships through life.

I bring this up because these thoughts capture the general idea in the world today about marriage. Fewer people are getting married, while divorce rates are at an all-time high. And Christians are not immune to this alarming trend because of the pervasive ignorance of what marriage is.

Although the article closes with an appeal to redefine what marriage is, it takes a swipe at the church for taking a stand against divorce.

The preacher Dr. Myles Munroe said, "When purpose is not known, abuse is inevitable." There, indeed, lies the problem with our idea about marriage. The purpose of marriage is relatively unknown to most people. This is evidenced by the prevalence of domestic violence, infidelity, and the climbing divorce rates globally.

When most people marry, they marry for love, money, or both. But that's not what marriage is fundamentally about. Marriage is about divine expression. Feminists may disagree with this assertion and dismiss it as patriarchal. They would be right to do so in the context of women and men because a woman should not have to derive her identity from marrying a man and bearing his name, as is the case in most parts of the world. However, with a wife, it is different—and here is the tricky part. A wife is one with her husband in such a sense that they, as a married couple, are not two partners connecting on a spiritual, emotional, and physical level based on a marriage certificate. They are one—an entirely new being that did not exist before their marriage.

Marriage Reveals the Image of God

The Bible is very clear on this when it says, "So God created man in his own image, in the image of God created he him; male and female created he them" (Genesis 1:27).

The image of God is both male and female, and this image finds its fullest expression every time a man joins a woman in the context of marriage. To corroborate this, Jesus said:

> From the beginning of the creation God made them "male and female". For this cause shall a man leave his father and mother, and cleave to his wife; and they twain shall be one flesh: so then they are no more twain, but one flesh. What, therefore, God hath joined together, let not man put asunder. (Mark 10:6–9)

In essence, men and women are designed with an innate desire for each other. And this desire, however fulfilled, is what marriage is.

Given this, it is worthy to note that there is no such thing as premarital sex or sex before marriage. The scriptures are replete with the indication that to have sex with someone is to be married to that person. "What? know ye not that he which is joined to a harlot is one body? For two, says he, shall be one flesh" (1 Corinthians 6:16). This idea forms the basis for common-law marriage in certain parts of the world in which cohabiting is legally recognized as marriage. In other parts, a marriage isn't recognized as valid until it has been consummated via sexual intercourse. Simply put, sex is marriage.

Marriage Is God's Witness of Christ to the World

A second idea that supports the relevance of marriage in our day is that it bears witness of Christ to the world. Marriage, in its most perfect state, epitomises the kind of relationship God desires to have with the whole world. Paul, the apostle, draws a direct relationship between husband and wife and Christ and the church, as he wrote about marital responsibilities in his letter to the Ephesians.

At Christ Community Chapel on April 12, 2015, Christian writer, Ravi Zacharias said, while taking part in a question-and-answer session on his book, *Answering the Biggest Objections to Christianity*, "Marriage—as God has given it to us and if you take the whole corpus of the worldview—is the most sacred relationship into which you will enter."

His premise is two-fold—the first being that marriage is the only human relationship that captures the essence of love. The Bible tells us, "God is love." But no human relationship displays this love—that God is—like a marriage does. The English language has just one word for love, but there are four words in the Greek—*agape, phileo, storge,* and *eros*—that capture the different ramifications of love.

- *Agape*, meaning "the God kind of love or unconditional love."
- *Phileo*, meaning "brotherly love or friendly love."

- *Storge*, meaning "love between a parent and a child."
- *Eros*, meaning "romantic love or intimate love."

And while all of this ties into the previous idea that marriage is the projection of God's image, it is also a powerful witness to the world about the love that exists between Christ and His church. In the epistles, Paul writes, "Husbands, love your wives, even as Christ also loved the Church, and gave himself for it" (Ephesians 5:25). This is Ravi Zacharias's second premise—that if a man or woman can identify the ramifications of unconditionality, friendship, kin, and intimacy encapsulated in the love of married couples, then the essence of Christianity is within grasp.

Like a bailiff serving court notices, marriage—no matter what part of the worldview you approach it from—notifies us all of love in its purest form—the love of Christ. Romans 5:7–8 (New International Version) reads thus, "*Very rarely will anyone die for a righteous person, though for a good person someone might possibly dare to die. But God demonstrates his own love for us in this: while we were still sinners, Christ died for us.*" Many at the Day of Judgment may claim that they never did have a chance at grasping the gospel of Jesus Christ, but marriage will stand as one of the witnesses against them.

Marriage Is the Only Guaranteed Foundation for the Human Society

To say that marriage is an antiquated tradition is to invalidate its importance to the human society, even at a primal level. Every human society derives its essence from the family. As Pope John XXIII said, "The family is the first essential cell of the human society." The family derives its being from the coming together of husband and wife in matrimony. It always has, and it always will.

Leaning backward to the suggestion that adults consider having several sexual relationships during the course of their lives based on what phase they are in is more devilish than sociological. First, it presupposes that marriage was artificially created by us and, so, can be done away with at will; second, that marriage was not part of our original design like other basic functions like walking, breathing, and making love. But neither is true.

We see from scripture that when God made marriage, He made it with an intent in mind. He made it to harmonize the components of a male and a female—husband and wife—into one creation, representative of His image and incapable of dissolution except by death. We also know that God made marriage as a means for man to execute his God-given dominion mandate.

> *So God created man in his own image, in the image of God created he him; male and female created he them. And God blessed them, and God said unto them, be fruitful, and multiply, and fill the earth, and subdue it: and have dominion over the fish of the sea, and over the fowl of the air, and over every living thing that moves upon the earth.*
> (Genesis 1:27–28)

It is striking how the first audience of human beings that God spoke to were a husband and wife. And though one might delineate the creation account in Genesis 1 from the formation account in Genesis 2, it is imperative to note that the first human relationship to be revealed in Scripture was a marriage.

God purpose-built marriage to be His image here on earth, which is why—unbeknownst to many—human beings marry, irrespective of race, culture, and creed. Therefore, it appears that to fully grasp marriage, one must first get a glimpse into God's character and the inherent ramifications thereof.

- *God does not make mistakes.*

    He set up a system for blessing humanity, and that system remains a marriage.

    > *And God blessed them, and God said unto them, be fruitful, and multiply, and fill the earth, and subdue it: and have dominion over the fish of*

the sea, and over the fowl of the air, and over every living thing that moves upon the earth. (Genesis 1:28)

For society to thrive, it must be based on God's system of spiritual, emotional, mental, and physical intercourse between a husband and wife, who produce good fruit, multiply, replenish, and subdue their environment with the blessing of their fruitfulness.

- *God does not change His mind about His personality.*

It is not in God's character to change His mind about His image. Malachi 3:6 says, "I am the *Lord*, I change not." In essence, God is saying, "I am the same." And this is the reason I believe God hates divorce, according to Malachi 2:16. Divorce is a distortion of His image.

- *God is purpose-driven, not event-driven.*

It is God's character to be purpose-driven. Isaiah 46:10 (NIV) gives us a snapshot of this quality: "I make known the end from the beginning, from ancient times, what is still to come. I say, 'My purpose will stand, and I will do all that I please.'" This shows up in marriage, too, in the sense that God's purpose, where marriage is concerned, is to project His image in the fullest manner possible. This purpose applies to Christian and non-Christian marriages, even though Christians may better appreciate it with proper knowledge and application of Scripture. As the New Living Translation of Proverbs 19:21 puts it, "You can make many plans, but the *Lord's* purpose will prevail." Even though a marriage will pass through different phases—some tough and others not so daunting—as it runs its course, only couples with hearts firmly latched onto God's purpose of mirroring His image to the world will be able to do so with intensity, pleasing the Father.

Going back to the question, Is marriage an outdated tradition? The simple answer is no. It appears from Scripture, nature, and the whole corpus of the worldview that marriage, in every way, bears a timeless sacredness that cannot be masked by the sociological position, which loosely postulates that marriage is a partnership or the climbing appetite for divorce that it supports. And yes, marriage is not a partnership. You read right. But I will discuss the subject in greater detail as you read on.

Chapter 3

The Unresolved Problem

The main and most difficult problem of marriage has not yet been resolved. As I wrote in the preceding chapter, the biggest problem is knowledge, even though many think it is love.

Love is not the basis for marriage. We usually get married because we say we are in love. And this is all right, but what we call love is actually appreciation, which I will talk about later. After being married myself for more than a decade, I can say that what we call love doesn't make marriage work. Do not be fooled by the *Oxytocin Phase*, which is characterized by the butterflies you feel in your stomach anytime you are with that man or woman—the endearment you feel toward your significant other—because it will pass.

It is not the lack of love that is the problem but the lack of knowledge. Looking at the subject of marriage from the viewpoint of separated or divorced couples more keenly, you will realize that it wasn't the absence of love that led to the breakdown. If you are separated or divorced right now—except under special circumstances where a spouse was arranged for you and you never really felt any form of appreciation—you will agree that you were once in love and, probably, are still in love with the person you were once married to. So you didn't lack love. Rather, there were some issues that arose in the marriage that your love couldn't deal with. It might have been infidelity, physical abuse, emotional abuse, neglect, or financial mismanagement. Something came up that shrouded the love you had for this person.

Speaker and author, Dr. Myles Munroe insisted that, "Successful marriage is the result of the application of knowledge, not the exchange of love."

Married couples can be in love all they want—it does not make any difference. Only knowledge can make marriage invulnerable to collapse. Your love will not transform your spouse into the right man or woman. This is why the Bible in Proverbs 4:7 says, "Wisdom is the principal thing; therefore get wisdom: and with all thy getting, get understanding." Essentially, wisdom is the first requirement in a marriage. You get wisdom, and with wisdom, you get understanding. You ought to know what it is to be a husband or a wife, what governs the demeanor of a male or female, the intricacies of communication, how to manage anger, exercise patience, build trust, handle unfaithfulness, and so on. Understanding what a marriage is and how a marriage works should be foremost for intending and married couples; otherwise, the union could be doomed.

Many marriages, ending in divorce, could have been saved if only the spouses engaged are knowledgeable on its precepts. They did not have the knowledge to work through their differences and wound up before a judge they had no business being in front of. No marriage is beyond redemption. However, not knowing how to solve problems can make them fester until the couple decides to call it quits. And honestly, problems can wear you out and make you tire of your marriage. They can rob you of happiness, money, and your sense of worth so that all you think about is the emergency exit called divorce. This is why it is important to get knowledge.

Hosea 4:6 says, "*My people are destroyed for lack of knowledge: because thou hast rejected knowledge, I will also reject thee, that thou shalt be no priest to me: seeing thou hast forgotten the law of thy God, I will also forget thy children.*" But here is the part we never really notice, where it says, "You have rejected knowledge, I will also reject you."

In other words, your ignorance is totally of your own making. And the vital thing to consider is that you cannot reject something that isn't available to you. Ignorance is, therefore, a personal choice and a damning decision we make as married couples. The books we refuse to read, the audio programs we refuse to listen to, and the seminars we refuse to attend all constitute a deliberate proclivity for ignorance. Well, ignorance has its consequences. The Bible says that God rejects those who reject knowledge. Imagine the many times you have felt alone in your marriage. Now you know why.

Another consequence of rejecting knowledge that the Lord talks about in Hosea 4:6 is that those who refuse to be knowledgeable cannot be His representatives. That is what He meant when He said, "You shall be no priest before me."

We have seen that it is not in God's character to leave Himself without witness and that marriage was designed to project the image of God, to represent Him on earth. Therefore, we understand from this scripture that God cannot abide a novice for the reason that novices are a threat to His reputation. Marriage is exactly this kind of rejected priesthood to God when you and your spouse choose to be ignorant of His Word on marriage.

The Case of Eli

One of the most profound stories of God, rejecting one of His priests, is that of Eli. Born a direct descendant of Aaron into a family chosen and charged by God with the responsibility of looking after the Ark of the Covenant and carrying out priestly duties, Eli was the first and only one to ever serve as both priest and judge, double-hatting the offices of spiritual and military leader of Israel.

Eli also had leadership over his two sons, Hopni and Phinehas, who themselves had entered the priesthood and were his protégés in the ministry. Yet, in all of these capacities of leadership that Eli occupied, there were many signs to show his constant and willful rejection of the Word of God, coupled with his dereliction of duty. This is obvious from the Bible's description of Eli's time as priest as a time when the Word of the Lord was rare and visions were infrequent (1 Samuel 3:1). The Word of God ought not to have been rare since

God had a priest in office, but it was. This is the first indictment of Eli's priesthood.

Reading the rest of 1 Samuel 3, we find that Eli is indicted against God's call of Samuel. First, Samuel does not realize that God is the one calling him until Eli discerns it and teaches him how to respond to God. This means that Eli knew how to receive divine instructions and, maybe, like many husbands and wives today, had become too familiar with the Word of God. Maybe their spouse cheated for the umpteenth time, and they are not having it anymore. They decide on divorcing each other.

"After all, the Bible allows couples to divorce on grounds of infidelity, doesn't it?" you ask. It does, but this is not God's best way for resolution of such problems. God's preference for resolution is that you forgive seventy times seven. His second best is divorce. And really, it isn't as if God can stomach divorce because the Bible also says that He hates divorce. God only allowed divorce because of the hardness of the human heart (Mark 10:4–6). Heart here refers to your spirit, not the organ beating in your chest. A hard heart or spirit, as we know it, is:

- Unregenerate
- Unforgiving
- Impatient
- Presumptuous
- Impermeable

Christians don't have a human heart. We have a new heart from the Lord. Speaking to Prophet Ezekiel in the Old Testament, the Lord said of the church, *"I will give you a new heart and put a new spirit in you; I will remove from you your heart of stone and give you a heart of flesh"* (Ezekiel 36:26 NIV).

We receive this new heart the moment we are born again because, in that moment as well, our hearts are infused with the love of God by the Holy Spirit (see Romans 5:5). We no longer have a heart that looks to divorce as an alternative to resolving conflict in a marriage but a heart that forgives, perseveres, and hopes. It is why

God expects us to "be kind to one another, tender-hearted, forgiving each other, just as God in Christ also has forgiven you" (Ephesians 4:32). He has put His love in our hearts so that we are capable of being kind to our spouses, of being affectionate toward them, and of being forgiving, just as God forgave us in Christ. There is absolutely nothing you cannot endure or forgive with a heart that has been tenderized by the love of God.

The second thing we learn from Samuel's encounter with God in 1 Samuel 3 is Eli's presumptuousness. Even after he had been warned by the Lord about the consequences of the abuse perpetrated by his sons, who had become accustomed to stealing offerings and sleeping with women at the temple, Eli did nothing sufficient to put a stop to it. In a sense, God had indicted Eli as an accomplice to his children's philandering for failure to act appropriately with the Word of God. This attitude to the knowledge of God's Word is what has brought about the soaring divorce rate in Christendom. "Husbands, love your wives as Christ loved the Church" and "Wives, submit to your own husbands" have been met with an unresponsiveness that has led many to blaspheme the name of the Lord.

Here is something to note: husband and wife are priestly offices instituted by God to project His image to the world so that the peoples of this world are without excuse. If you are a husband or a wife, know this: God is not always going to speak to you about how to conduct your marriage particularly if He already has done so through the scriptures. More often than not and as a matter of duty, you are going to have to reach out to Him by studying the Bible and spending time in prayer if His blessings are going to be evident in your marriage. To do otherwise is to jeopardize your marriage as Eli jeopardized his posterity. Even though Eli lived to be ninety-eight, the repercussion of ignoring God's Word was so grave that it cut the life span of his entire generation so that none of them would ever live to old age (see 1 Samuel 4:17–18).

The worst consequence of ignoring the Word of God is that the children—whether they be spiritual or biological—endure the worst of it, and marriage is no exception. Nowhere do children suffer more, aside from war, than in a marriage that has collapsed. From the logistic nightmare of child custody and co-parenting arrangements to the toxicity of being raised by a father and mother, who no longer love each other to the auto-suggestions about how they might have been the reason their parents got divorced in the first place—all of these conspire to make life hellish for children, sometimes well into adulthood. More troubling are studies which show that children of divorce are more likely to divorce, having picked up their parents' relationship skills and attitudes to marital commitment.

Hosea 4:6 sums up these generational consequences of choosing ignorance. If you do not learn how to stay married and get it right, your children may also be in danger of suffering the same problem. Reading books, listening to podcasts or audio programs, and attending seminars on the subject of marriage can significantly improve your relationship with your spouse so that your marriage fulfills its destiny, projects the image of God, and influences your children for Christ in the way that God intended for it to.

Think of knowledge as something that comes with the terrain of marriage. Until you are in communication with the Lord through prayer and Bible study, reading books, and/or attending seminars on marriage as a lifestyle, marital problems are bound to remain unresolved. It has nothing to do with the person you marry and everything to do with knowledge. Marrying him or her may have been a mistake, but God never intended for your marriage to end in divorce. Like a GPS in a car, God can help you and your spouse recalibrate your way to joy and fulfillment. After all, does the Bible not say that all things work together for good to them that love God and are called according to His purpose?

You may, even now, be in love with someone else, thinking this person trumps your spouse in many ways. Without knowledge, even if you divorce your spouse to marry this other person, it will only be a matter of time before the new marriage collapses. Statistics support this: divorced people are more likely to divorce in subsequent marriages if the problem of knowledge remains unresolved.

Do not quit your marriage, except if the Lord permits you to do so through the appropriate spiritual counsel. Know this: God did not design marriage to end in divorce but in death. Moreover, even if it feels like hell right now, it is because you have allowed the lack of knowledge to remain the unresolved problem.

A Final Word

The pundits say that Christians are divorcing as rapidly as non-Christians, and though there is no way to verify this, one can tell that it is probably because we, in the body of Christ, aren't using what we have—the knowledge of God's Word.

The Bible is full of stories about how we are so different from the rest of the world. Remember, the waters that buoyed Noah's boat were the same in which the rest of the world perished. Likewise, our marriages ought not to be as the marriages of those outside our faith.

But nothing better captures the idea of the unresolved problem of the Christian marriage like Proverbs 11:9 (English Standard Version):

"With his mouth the godless man would destroy his neighbor, but by knowledge the righteous are delivered."

Chapter 4

No Longer Two but One

Seeing that knowledge is the secret to a successful marriage, it is necessary to register a fundamental truth about marriage, which has been grossly overlooked through the years: *Marriage is not a partnership but a union.*

I know that you have heard all your life, from people from all walks of life, how husband and wife are partners. Systematically, we have been brainwashed into thinking and behaving as though husband and wife are partners, but nothing violates God's idea of marriage more than this. Husband and wife are not partners but components—parts joined together to form a whole. And though many could easily water down my meaning to mere semantics, many marriages—even the ones that seem to be thriving—slip up at this partnership/union dichotomy.

According to the *Merriam-Webster's Dictionary*, a *partnership* is "a legal relation existing between two or more persons contractually associated as joint principals in a business." A partnership connotes the idea of the coming together of two or more people for a common purpose or ideal.

In the context of marriage as a partnership, the larger worldview today recognizes it as the coming together of two individuals—irrespective of gender—to formalize, by a marriage license, their desire to be together, no matter what the reasons are: love, money, commonality, or heritage. This idea of partnership also comes with the inherent idea of dissolubility—that a marriage as was contracted could also be dissolved at the instance of any partner for any reason at all, revealing its true source.

Men and women have been conditioned to think this way by the devil for the very reason that marriage reminds him of God and of his ultimate future. Satan is the source of the thinking that marriage is a partnership because, with it, he has been able to steer mankind away from God's dominion mandate. It is this thinking that has produced the quantum upsurge in divorces that we see across the world today—that marriage is a two-or-more people affair, which it is not.

God's viewpoint of marriage is that a man and his wife are "no longer two but one." Let us look at Mark 10:2–9:

> *The Pharisees came and asked Him, "Is it lawful for a man to divorce his wife?" testing Him. And He answered and said to them, "What did Moses command you?" They said, "Moses permitted a man to write a certificate of divorce, and to dismiss her." And Jesus answered and said to them, "Because of the hardness of your heart he wrote you this precept.*
> BUT FROM THE BEGINNING OF THE CREATION, GOD 'MADE THEM MALE AND FEMALE. FOR THIS REASON A MAN SHALL LEAVE HIS FATHER AND MOTHER AND BE JOINED TO HIS WIFE, AND THE TWO SHALL BECOME ONE FLESH'; SO THEN THEY ARE NO LONGER TWO, BUT ONE FLESH. THEREFORE WHAT GOD HAS JOINED TOGETHER, LET NOT MAN SEPARATE."

God created humankind and, by extension, marriage to be His harmonized image. The emphasized portion in the scripture above, where Jesus references two other portions of scripture in the Book of Genesis, can help us with insights into God's intent for marriage in the beginning.

Genesis 1:26–28:

> *Then God said, "Let Us make man in Our image, according to Our likeness; let them have dominion over the fish of the sea, over the birds of the air, and over the cattle, over all the earth and over every creeping thing that creeps on the earth." So God created man in His own image; in the image of God He created him; male and female He created them. Then God blessed them, and God said to them, "Be fruitful and multiply; fill the earth and subdue it; have dominion over the fish of the sea, over the birds of the air, and over every living thing that moves on the earth."*

Genesis 2:21–25

> *And the Lord God caused a deep sleep to fall on Adam, and he slept; and He took one of his ribs, and closed up the flesh in its place. Then the rib which the Lord God had taken from man He made into a woman, and He brought her to the man. And Adam said: "This is now bone of my bones and flesh of my flesh; she shall be called Woman, because she was taken out of Man." Therefore a man shall leave his father and mother and be joined to his wife, and they shall become one flesh. And they were both naked, the man and his wife, and were not ashamed.*

Although Mark 10:2–9 emphasizes everything we need to know about how God sees marriage, Genesis 1:26–28 and 2:21–25 granulate them so that the oneness of marriage is unearthed in the following points:

> a) God created humankind, male and female, to manifest His image. It is evident, all through the Bible, that God has both male and female qualities and chose to separate these qualities in man and woman so that husband and wife would have to rely on each other in the execution of their assignment.
> b) Marriage was fashioned to be the vehicle for husband and wife to fulfill their God-given assignment on earth. It is important to note that every marriage has a specific assignment or group of assignments from God, which is why a couple must first be acquainted with God and their assignment during the course of their marriage or, preferably, before they marry.
> c) When a man and a woman become husband and wife, they are no longer two individuals but one, having all things in common with nothing to be ashamed about. And here's the tricky part: there can be no secrets between them because they are now sharers in one life.

The temerity with which Jesus tells us of the relevance of marriage in Mark 10:2–9 goes far beyond any sociological or psychological positions because He was there at the beginning and had a grasp of why marriage was designed in the first place.

All of men's theorizing that marriage is unnatural, that human beings evolved from bonobos and that bonobos were polygamous, often having children with as many of their species as possible, is plausible but holds no bearing with Jesus's account of the beginning. The very cloth from which marriage is cut communicates a husband and wife becoming a whole new person the moment they become mature enough to leave and cleave.

It is this same singularity of truth that trails up from the Book of Genesis to the gospels and then to the epistles, where Paul, the apostle, uses it to teach the mystery of Christ and His church; the purest marriage of all—that a man leaves his father and mother and becomes joined to his wife so that the two of them become one flesh (see Genesis 2:24, Matthew 19:5, and Ephesians 5:31). The chief suggestion that is given from the mystery of Christ and His church is that the whole point of Jesus leaving the Father in heaven, coming to the earth to live as a man, being crucified and then being raised on the third day was to become one with us, His believers, so that we couldn't be told apart from Him.

But let's not get ahead of ourselves with this idea. Let's look at a few scriptures again.

Ephesians 5:22–33:

> *Wives, submit to your own husbands, as to the Lord. For the husband is head of the wife, as also Christ is head of the church; and He is the Saviour of the body. Therefore, just as the church is subject to Christ, so let the wives be to their own husbands in everything.*
>
> *Husbands, love your wives, just as Christ also loved the church and gave Himself for her, that He might sanctify and cleanse her with the washing of water by the word, that He might present her to Himself a glorious church, not having spot or wrinkle or any such thing, but that she should be holy and without blemish.*
>
> SO HUSBANDS OUGHT TO LOVE THEIR OWN WIVES AS THEIR OWN BODIES; HE WHO LOVES HIS WIFE LOVES HIMSELF. FOR NO ONE EVER HATED HIS OWN FLESH, BUT NOURISHES AND CHERISHES IT, JUST AS THE LORD DOES THE CHURCH. FOR WE ARE MEMBERS OF HIS BODY, OF HIS FLESH AND OF HIS BONES.
>
> *For this reason a man shall leave his father and mother and be joined to his wife, and the two shall become one flesh. This is a great mystery, but I speak concerning Christ and the church. Nevertheless let*

each one of you in particular so love his own wife as himself, and let the wife see that she respects her husband.

If you are already married, perish the thought, today, that your spouse is your partner. Your spouse is a part of you, just as you are a part of Christ, assuming you are a Christian. If you are not yet married, marriage means taking on a new part or becoming part of the person you marry, which, in the beginning, could feel a bit awkward until you become accustomed to the uses or usage of that part. That is the reason for most of the conflicts in marriage. It is also the reason why the Bible is very particular about the word *submission* in Ephesians 5:22–33. We will deal with the subject of submission later on.

Grafting comes to mind when attempting to describe what the oneness of marriage is.

In horticulture, this is a common practice that entails fusing the tissues of two similar species together for the purpose of creating a new species of plant. One plant is selected for its roots and is called the rootstock. The other plant is selected for its stem, branches, flowers, or fruit and is called the scion.

Like the human marriage, the tissues of the rootstock and scion must be joined and kept alive for a time until the graft has taken place. Unfortunately, many marriages never last long enough for husbands and wife to manifest or even realize their oneness.

A grafting is only successful once a vascular connection is established between the tissues of the rootstock and the scion. The two parts become one plant in function, particularly in the ability to bear fruit. Horticulturists call this point the inosculation, and though we have no way of truly pinpointing when an inosculation occurs between husband and wife, the Jesus message, "Not two but one," sums it all up.

Chapter 5

The Birthplace of Divorce

Genesis 29:21–35 tells the story of Leah—her forced marriage to Jacob, her having to endure his preference for another woman, who happened to be her sister, and her giving birth to four boys in quick succession. This passage prophetically pinpoints the place of inosculation—where the husband and wife actually realize their oneness.

Inosculation happens when a husband and a wife mutually realize the different ramifications of their commitment to each other. Understanding the ramifications of the marriage commitment is like the tissues of scion and rootstock finally making that vital vascular connection in grafting, which makes the scion and the rootstock one plant. The deduction, then, is that if this mutuality of understanding is not reached in time, like a failed grafting, the marriage may also never be vital, even if the couple decide to stay together.

The Need for Validation

Using Leah's first four childbirths as milestones, the Bible tells us that God saw that Leah was hated and decided to bless her by opening up her womb. The first child He blessed her with, she named Reuben, meaning "behold a son." She said, "Now therefore, my husband will love me." Reuben's birth signified a need for validation because she thought that, if she gave Jacob a son, he would validate her as his wife.

The first tissues that seek vascular connection in a new marriage grafting are those of validation. "This is my husband" and "this is my wife." The recognition that you are no longer partners—boyfriend and girlfriend—but components of each other—husband and wife—is a significant shift both of you must make in private and, of course, in public. There can be no fusion until each of you validate the other for who they are in the union. Many very young couples affected by societal expectations, perhaps because of their age, often fall through the cracks by not validating each other enough.

For couples marrying older, there is a constant lure to validate each other based on accomplishments—be they financial or professional. This, again, is based on the societal expectation that one should have experienced some financial or professional success anywhere between the ages of thirty-five and sixty-five. However, validating your spouse because of their accomplishments should be occasional rather than the norm. We validate our spouses for who they are, not necessarily for what they accomplish. The idea behind validating your spouse for who he or she is to you is something that cannot be overemphasized because when you truly do so, you express acceptance for your spouse with the fundamental knowledge that he or she is a part of you.

Many people do not particularly make the mental transition from singleness to being married, much of the reason being societal expectations. If this is you, a good way to solve this problem is to practice validation. A few more times each day, refer to your spouse as "my wife" or "my husband" to her or his hearing. The import of this practice is that it registers in your subconscious mind until it becomes second nature.

The Need to Be Listened To

Then the Lord blessed Leah with a second child, and she called him Simeon, meaning "listened to." Simeon's birth represented a desire to be listened to or be heard. The second vascular connection that makes a husband and wife become one in marriage is being listened to. The art of listening to your spouse is so pivotal to attaining oneness that couples may need to hone their listening skills very early; otherwise, their marriage may be prone to trouble. The way to your spouse's heart is through your ears. When spouses can pour their hearts out to each other without judgment, oneness does not require rocket science. It simply happens.

The Need for a Sense of Belonging

Next, Leah had Levi. She named him so because of a desire for commitment. The name Levi, meaning "to be joined," signified a need to have a sense that she belonged with her husband, to share a commonality that the marital union was designed for. And so, the third vascular connection that needs to be established between a husband and a wife, in order to realize their oneness, is a sense of belonging to each other. And this is the thing that matters most in any marriage—recognizing that your spouse, in the words of Adam, is "bone of your bone and flesh of your flesh" (see Genesis 2:23).

This is the final connection that makes a marriage reach the inosculation point that God designed marriage to. In every sense of the word, this is what the Bible means in 1 Peter 3:7 (Berean Study Bible), where it says, "Husbands, treat your wives with consideration as a delicate vessel, and with honour as fellow heirs of the gracious gift of life, so that your prayers will not be hindered." While some Bible translations of this portion of scripture have sparked all kinds of gender-based acrimony, which in itself is needless, what the Bible actually says here of the wife is that she is a delicate part of the union, to be treated with consideration and honour, not just because she is a delicate part—and we all know the care and honour we give the delicate parts of our body in our personal grooming—but because she is also a joint signatory to the life we live on earth, determining, together with her husband, what benefits they both receive from the Lord.

Marriage by divine design is beautiful, but like the relationship between the scion and the rootstock in grafting, it could be prone to failure if the painstaking attention required to make it work is somehow overlooked in our bid to conform to society or just out of sheer carelessness. Even I am not a professor at this yet, to be honest with you. But what is guaranteed to make a marriage work is the husband and wife resolving with oneness of mind to validate, listen to, and be part of each other in the manner that God designed them to be. Someone may say they made a mistake choosing a spouse—and I will get to this soon enough—but that's not what the Bible says. The scriptures say it was God who joined you both. You, and every one of us, are duty bound to never separate what God has joined.

Finally, Leah gave birth to Judah and then left bearing children. It is very symbolic that she left bearing children after Judah because Judah is the representation of the God-predetermined destination for marriage. Leah's other children may have represented the journey, but Judah is God's end point for every marriage. *Judah* means "praise."

As I mentioned earlier, marriage is the only relationship that *expresses the image of God in high-definition picture so that men are without excuse about His person.* "*So God created man in His own image; in the image of God He created him; male and female He created them*" (Genesis 1:27).

If, on the Day of Judgment, some people say they never had the opportunity to hear the gospel and surrender their lives to God, marriage will bear witness that they did understand the relationship God wanted to have with them all through their time on earth. The first people God formed and described as being in His image were a husband and wife. The first miracle that Jesus performed, manifesting the glory of God, was at a wedding (see John 2:11). And the first act of the Holy Spirit after the death and burial of the Lord Jesus was to raise us up together with Him (see Acts 2 and Ephesians 2:6)—in essence, formalizing the purest marriage ever known of Christ and His church.

Now, Leah did have other children with Jacob, but her other children—Issachar, Zebulun, and Dinah—represent separate significance after the point of inosculation when the husband and wife have become one—in mind and body.

Marriage Is for Praise

Marriage has always been God's vehicle for humanity to praise Him. For instance, the Bible says that, "Out of the mouth of children, God has ordained praise" (see Matthew 21:16). Children come from marriages. And I don't care whether organized religion says a child was born out of wedlock or not. The moment a man and a woman carnally know each other, that is a marriage. "And Adam knew Eve his wife" (Genesis 4:1).

Our marriage to the Lord, being Christians, is no different. The Bible says of us, the bride of Christ, that we are a chosen people, a royal priesthood, and a holy nation. To what end? To show forth the praises of the one who called us out of darkness into His marvelous light (see 1 Peter 2:9).

If you have gotten to this point and do not see why Satan hates marriage, you might as well pack it in and stop reading. But I think you do, so please continue.

Failed Grafting

Grafting procedures, whether horticultural (between the scion and rootstock of plants) or dermatological (skin-to-skin) do fail sometimes. And then, the procedures have to be redone with the consciousness of what went wrong that made the prior procedure fail.

Marriages can be like this too, only the signs of failure to become one are very difficult to spot until, perhaps, it is too late and divorce seems imminent. But what really happens that turns couples, who were once in love enough to get married into conflicted components, now repulsed by the idea of being one?

Jesus answers this question succinctly: the hardness of our hearts.

Speaking to the Pharisees, who had come to test Him on His knowledge of divorce laws of that day, the conversation went thus:

> *"Don't you read the Scriptures?" he replied. "In them it is written that at the beginning God created man and woman, and that a man should leave his father and mother, and be forever united to his wife. The two shall become one—no longer two, but one! And no man may divorce what God has joined together."*
>
> *"Then, why," they asked, "did Moses say a man may divorce his wife by merely writing her a letter of dismissal?"*
>
> *Jesus replied, "Moses did that in recognition of your hard and evil hearts, but it was not what God had originally intended. And I tell you this, that anyone who divorces his wife, except for fornication, and marries another, commits adultery."*
>
> (Matthew 19:4–9 Living Bible TLB)

The Hard and Evil Heart

Divorce originates out of a hard and evil heart. It is the kind of heart that, if just one spouse possesses, the grafting fails. This heart refuses to validate, listen to, or see yourself as part of your spouse. The Bible qualifies it as a heart of unbelief, hardened by the deceitfulness of sin (see Hebrews 3:12–13). It is a self-centred and prideful heart.

For us Christians, we have to be neck-deep in the world to ever manifest the attributes of a hard and evil heart. Why? Because we do not have this kind of heart. In the Old Testament, God promised that He would remove this hard and evil heart from among His people and replace it with a pliable heart.

In Ezekiel 36:26–27, God said:

> *I will give you a new heart and put a new spirit within you; I will take the heart of stone out of your flesh and give you a heart of flesh. I will put My Spirit within you and cause you to walk in My statutes, and you will keep My judgments and do them.*

We know that God fulfilled His promise for three reasons. God set a new standard of love (see John 13:34–35 and Romans 13:8–10). Then He broadcast His love in our hearts through the Holy Ghost that now resides in us (see Romans 5:5). Finally, He instructs us to "*be kind to one another, tender-hearted, forgiving one another, even as God in Christ forgave you*" (Ephesians 4:32). We know that God never instructs a person to do something without first giving them the capacity to do it.

What Ephesians 4:32 tells us is that Christians have the actual capacity to be kind, tenderhearted, and forgiving in the same manner as God, which He demonstrated when He forgave us in Christ.

Now if Christians have a tender heart from God, why then do Christians get divorced? Why are there statistics about Christians divorcing in similar fashion as the rest of the world? Jesus said Moses allowed divorce because of the hardness of men's hearts. In other words, divorce originates from a hard heart. But we are new persons in Christ with new hearts that are capable of manifesting the undiluted love of God. So, what happens?

A Seared Conscience

Many Christians develop what is known as a seared conscience. A seared conscience is a hardening of the Christian heart or spirit after it has been tenderized at the new birth. The conscience is the receptacle of the human spirit. The conscience is how the human spirit distinguishes right from wrong or good from evil. The other word *sear* means "to burn or char an opened surface in order to seal up." Essentially, a seared conscience is a conscience that can no longer distinguish between right and wrong.

1 Timothy 4:1–3 deconstructs the origin, idea, and machinations of a seared conscience. It says:

> *Now the Spirit expressly says that in latter times some will depart from the faith, giving heed to deceiving spirits and doctrines of demons, speaking lies in hypocrisy, having their own conscience seared with a hot iron, forbidding to marry, and commanding to abstain from foods which God created to be received with thanksgiving by those who believe and know the truth.*

A seared conscience is one of the signs of a departure from the faith of Jesus Christ. And one of the ways to detect a seared conscience is our attitude to marriage. Many spouses have given up their marriage because of a seared conscience. Do you ever wonder why, at the slightest occasion of adultery or some other problem, many resolve to divorce? It is a seared conscience. A seared conscience is the reason why the marriage grafting fails. It hinders connectivity between husband and wife in such a way that they can never become one—the way that God designed for them to be.

A Seared Conscience Is an Offended Conscience

The hot iron that sears the conscience is offense. Spouses, over time, are bound to have differences, particularly in the course of their becoming one. Sometimes, the offense may come from people or incidents prior to their marriage, which, allowed to linger, sears the conscience of one or both spouses so that the grafting process is impossible. In general, this is actually what people describe as irreconcilable differences, even if they don't realize it—the inability of a man and his wife to connect with each other the way God ordained for them to.

Offense primarily stems from unmet personal expectations that are often not communicated to the other person. In the marriage, they arise out of unmet expectations based on the three milestones—Reuben, Simeon, and Levi—mentioned earlier: validation from your spouse, being listened to by your spouse, and having a sense of belonging with him or her.

Offense also comes from unresolved emotional or psychological wounds or trauma. Many a man or woman—whose parents ended their marriage because of infidelity or physical abuse, endured rape, domestic violence or some other traumatic incident like the suicide of a family member—are held back from fully connecting with their spouses because they were offended by these happenings. For some, simply going back to this place prayerfully and asking the Lord to help you unpack it may be the turning point if you are experiencing any turbulence in your marriage.

According to my mentor and senior pastor of Grace House Church in Dayton, Ohio, Dr. Emmanuel Igbinoba, offense is an "odorless gas with the ability to inflict irrevocable damage on one's destiny if allowed to gain control."

The fact is that this is the origin of divorce at its very core. This is what sears the conscience and then hardens the heart so that the connecting tissues between spouses that were supposed to facilitate their fusion and sustain their marriage become blocked, eventually leading to the demise of the marriage.

Chapter 6

Supernatural

Someone once said, and I must concur, that "Christianity is nothing if it is not supernatural." And if I may add: "Marriage is nothing if it is not supernatural." It is not the wedding ceremony or the payment of bride price—as is the case in some climes—that finalizes marriage but the cleaving of a man to a woman, biologically speaking.

"And Adam knew Eve, his wife" (Genesis 4:1). This is the reason why adultery is the only biblical grounds for which a divorce may be sought by a spouse—even though forgiving an errant spouse has a far greater reward.

When a man and a woman have sex, they become one—bound together until death.

"*Or do you not know that he who is joined to a harlot is one body with her? For 'the two,' He says, 'shall become one flesh'*" (1 Corinthians 6:16).

This is why the Bible does not speak well of fornication. The idea is not to deprive us of sexual fulfillment but to prevent the catastrophic monstrosity that follows when people have sexual relations with others outside the confines of marriage.

The Christian marriage, therefore, points to an equal yoking and God's unceasing desire for equity and justice in everything He is involved in. The husband may be the head of his wife, but he is no more important than she is because of their oneness. They are both vital appendages of each other. Adam, on his first encounter with Eve, said, "This is now bone of my bones and flesh of my flesh; she shall be called Woman, because she was taken out of Man" (Genesis 2:23).

Cognizant of the fact that something supernatural had taken place when God tranquilized him and whipped out a woman from his side, Adam's attestation was not a show of superiority but an open acceptance of a part of himself that he had just become acquainted with. To put it succinctly, a wife is not subservient to her husband but a part of him as he is a part of her. In popular culture, this has not been the mindset because, somehow, husbands have not conditioned themselves to see their wives as a part of themselves. Nevertheless, it is no accident that the Bible uses the same figurative approach in describing both the church and marriage—albeit separately—as one body. Christ and husbands are the head, while the church and wives are the body.

I believe God allowed these references to be put in the Bible because of our sin-driven proclivity for institutionalizing natural and supernatural phenomena. Like the institutionalization of anything on earth, whether it be sports, entertainment, or even Christianity, the institutionalization of marriage was done over time to create commercial opportunities for a few. Yet, marriage is not an institution in its true essence. All through the Bible, marriage is a pulsating organism, capable of internal and external growth. Husband and wife are not the stoic partnership that mainstream media and organized religion have socialized us to accept—that the husband is the head and is, therefore, more important than the wife is. They are heirs together of the grace of life (1 Peter 3:7). They are one in design and function so that one is not more important than the other. After all, what is a head without a body?

Many have rightly construed Apostle Paul's message in 2 Corinthians 6:14 to mean Christians and non-Christians should not marry. This is correct. What they largely miss is why. The apostle follows up with five poignant questions that leave no doubt that marriage is supernatural. He comments:

> *Do not be unequally yoked together with unbelievers. For what fellowship has righteousness with lawlessness? And what communion has light with darkness? And what accord has Christ with Belial? Or what part has a believer with an unbeliever? And what agreement has the temple of God with idols? For you are the temple of the living God.* (2 Corinthians 6:14–16)

The reason why the person a Christian marries is so important is evident in the above scripture. It anchors the Christian's identity in Christ to who she/he should or should not marry for the same reasons that Paul asks:

- What fellowship has righteousness with lawlessness?
- What communion has light with darkness?
- What accord has Christ with Belial?
- What part has a believer with an unbeliever?
- What agreement has the temple of God with idols?

What fellowship has righteousness with lawlessness?

The word *fellowship*, used in this question, implies participation. In a sense, the apostle asks what participation would be fitting for a Christian married to an unbeliever. The scripture calls the Christian righteousness, not righteous. There is a reason for this. Righteousness qualifies a state of being, while righteous only qualifies a person. *Righteousness* is "the state of being right or aligned with God's rightness." In plainer terms, the Christian has met all of God's basic expectations for a human being.

The unbeliever, on the other hand, is described with the term *lawlessness*. Lawlessness, too, is a state of being. It is a state of being at variance with God. A person might be lawless for breaking the law, but when a person is lawlessness, she/he, at the core of personhood, is without God. Jesus puts the idea of lawlessness in proper perspective when He says:

> *Not everyone who says to me, "Lord, Lord," shall enter the kingdom of heaven, but he who does the will of My Father in heaven. Many will say to me in that day, "Lord, Lord, have we not prophesied in your name, cast out demons in your name, and done many wonders in your name?" And then I will declare to them, "I never knew you; depart from me, you who practice lawlessness!"* (Matthew 7:21–23)

The three parts of Jesus's statement in Matthew 7:23 surmise everything we need to know about lawlessness: '*I never knew you; depart from me, you who practice lawlessness!*'

First, God is unaccepting of lawlessness. It is inconsistent with his nature. Ephesians 2:12 reminds us that, while we were separate from Christ, we were in a state of exclusion from God and, by extension, exclusion from true hope.

Next, God cannot abide with lawlessness. This is the second thing Jesus's words indicate. Habakkuk 1:13 says that God is too pure to look on lawlessness or even condone lawless behavior. His nature abhors lawlessness for natural reasons. Lawlessness is a state of being that contradicts the nature of God the same way fresh water and salt water, meeting at an estuary, do not readily mix. The salt content in salt water makes it denser, causing the lighter fresh water to float above it.

The third thing, implicit in Jesus's statement, is that lawlessness leads to the perpetuation of lawless behavior. The compulsive liar or cheat cannot claim to be a Christian. The Christian may lie or cheat, but her true state of being, righteousness, holds her duty bound to act consistent with her true self. The unbeliever, therefore, acts consistent with his own true nature. He practices lawlessness. His participation in a marriage is subject to his nature. Married to a Christian spouse, both of them create an unequal yoking together that leans more toward lawlessness. After all, clean water mixed with unclean water becomes unclean. Like fresh water with salt water, which eventually mix, the unbelieving spouse is sanctified by the believing spouse (see 1 Corinthians 7:14). Their marriage will be a spiritual war zone for the same reason that the spiritual conditions of their lives are at variance with each other. What fellowship has righteousness with lawlessness?

What communion has light with darkness?

Communion is a very weighty word in Christendom. Its etymology emphasizes commonality more on a spiritual level than it does on psychic or physical planes. The root word, translated communion, occurs nine times in the Bible, each time pointed toward the Christian's supernatural commonality with the Father, the Holy Spirit, fellow believers, and our faith.

What commonality has light with darkness? John 1:5 (NIV) reads thus: "*The light shines in the darkness and the darkness has not overcome it.*" It suggests a discordant relationship between light and darkness in which the former is the ever-dominant aggressor, trouncing the latter each time they encounter each other.

Here, light is the archetypal good, while darkness is the archetypal evil. Jesus further clarifies this demarcation when He says, "I am the light of the world. He who follows me shall not walk in darkness, but have the light of life" (John 8:12). Followers of Jesus are the light, and non-followers grope in darkness.

As cliché as it sounds, light fulfills only one purpose: it propagates righteousness. Driving on Lombard Street in San Francisco, the most winding street in the world, at sixty miles an hour in the middle of the night, without crashing into anything, is only possible with good headlamps and streetlights, simply because light reveals that which is previously not seen and minimizes error.

Darkness, on the other hand, is a condition that supports lethargy. "The night comes when no man can work," Jesus says in John 9:4. In this regard, darkness has its usefulness, particularly with people who cannot seem to find any sleep until the lights are out.

Nevertheless, it is not in this context that the apostle asks the question about light and darkness. You see, just as light propagates righteousness, darkness propagates lawlessness, spiritually speaking.

Crime statistics show that more than two-thirds of rapes, muggings, and car thefts occur at night for the obvious reason that the underworld thrives under the cover of darkness.

Like a judge offering his verdict on the dichotomy between light and darkness, Jesus surmises:

> *Light has come into the world, but people loved darkness instead of light because their deeds were evil. Everyone who does evil hates the light, and will not come into the light for fear that their deeds will be exposed. But whoever lives by the truth comes into the light, so that it may be seen plainly that what they have done has been done in the sight of God.* (John 3:19–21 NIV)

Light can share no commonality with darkness in the same way that a Christian husband can share no spiritual commonality with his unbelieving wife. What commonality they could share is, at best, ephemeral, ring-fenced by the five senses so that God's idea for marriage never materializes in their union. Alternatively, the darkness present in their union opens the door to all kinds of demonic possibilities if the believing spouse has yet to come to terms with his or her identity in Christ: "*The light shines in the darkness, and the darkness has not overcome it.*"

What accord has Christ with Belial?

The word translated *accord* is the same root word from which the word *symphony* is derived. A more apt reframing of Paul's question would be, What vocal harmony has Christ with Belial?

To answer this question, one would first need to understand what vocal harmony is; following which, in the context of husband and wife, we will attempt to personify Christ and Belial.

A harmony is what you hear when two notes are played or sung simultaneously. Marriage is a spiritual song, requiring husband and wife to sing the notes simultaneously. This is why trifling things, such as the silent treatment, ought to be absent or at least minimized in a marriage relationship. Discordant tunes in marriage are certainly the biggest hindrance to answered prayer and unleashing the power of God in an area of desperate need. Maintaining the harmony of marriage rests on the resolve of both spouses to play their parts.

> *For in this manner, in former times, the holy women who trusted in God also adorned themselves, being submissive to their own husbands, as Sarah obeyed Abraham, calling him lord, whose daughters you are if you do good and are not afraid with any terror. Husbands, likewise, dwell with them with understanding, giving honour to the wife, as to the weaker vessel, and as being heirs together of the grace of life, that your prayers may not be hindered.* (1 Peter 3:5–7)

The feminist movement has not done justice to these verses of scripture, and for this reason, I feel a strong urge to reemphasize that the male-female dichotomy, by which many marriages operate, is not of God. Husband and wife are not partners but parts of each other. The woman and man parts of the union ought to submit to each other, going by the verses above and, in fact, the rest of the Bible.

First Peter 3:5–7 only tells the wife to submit to her own husband and not to other men. It tells the husband to facilitate his wife's submission by being cognizant of her views, which, in itself, is a form of submission. Again, charged with giving honor to his wife as his delicate part, the husband must observe another act of submission for the common good of the union. To give honor to a person is to bestow on them a sense of worth or belonging. The basic way to ascribe worth to a person is by listening to that person, valuing their contributions, and heeding their advice. A husband, therefore, honors his wife by listening to her and taking her opinions or contributions into full account for the overall advancement of their union. They sing the song of their union as one, with one voice every time.

Christ is the archetype of everything that embodies godliness. Christ is everything that Jesus was, is, and will be. Christ is also what believers of the gospel of Jesus Christ are. Jesus is the head, and His believers are His body. There can be no demarcation between Christ and the Christian because the Lord Himself identifies with His church in unalloyed terms. When Paul met Jesus for the first time on his way to Damascus to persecute Christians, having persecuted the church in Jerusalem to the point of overseeing the martyrdom of Stephen, the Lord of the universe introduced Himself with the words, "I am Jesus whom you are persecuting." This was in tandem with Jesus's parable of the sheep and goats, which implied that a deed done to a Christian is as one done to the Lord Jesus Himself. To crown it all, the believer takes on the brand name *Christ* in 1 Corinthians 6.

Belial, on the other hand, is the archetype of everything that embodies godlessness. Originally a Jewish word, signifying worthlessness, Belial came to refer to the devil personified. He is the diametric opposite of Christ in every shape, fashion, and form. What Christ is, Belial is not. What Christ loves, Belial hates. Christ raised from the dead what Belial killed. It is no wonder that men called *the sons of Belial* in the Bible represent the worst form of men because of their proclivity to sacrilege, wantonness, and destruction.

Harmony between Christ and Belial is not possible. The archetypal godly and the archetypal godless cannot produce a fitting denouement in marriage. Yet this is what Christians marrying unbelievers attempt. In hopes of somehow converting their intended spouses after the wedding, they produce the worst kind of dissonance in the realm of the spirit.

What part has a believer with an unbeliever?

Biblical Christianity (not as it is widely practiced today, pandering to denominationalism) suggests that Christians are parts of each other in a vital and pulsating way. We share an undeniable bond in Christ. Jesus is the vine, and we, His believers, are the branches. First Corinthians 12:12–14 paints this idea in the most easy-to-grasp picture:

> *Just as a body, though one, has many parts, but all its many parts form one body, so it is with Christ. For we were all baptized by one Spirit so as to form one body—whether Jews or Gentiles, slave or free— and we were all given the one Spirit to drink. Even so the body is not made up of one part but of many.*

The idea of being a part of something has more to do with usefulness than merely being a component of a whole. "Any branch in me that does not bear fruit, the Father cuts off," Jesus says (see John 15:2).

Productivity is, therefore, a derivative of one part's connectedness to other parts of the whole, which, in this instance, is a believing spouse with an unbelieving spouse. It acquiesces to the widely held fact first coined by the Greek philosopher Aristotle that the whole is greater than the sum of its parts. Nevertheless, it is noteworthy what happens when parts of a whole refuse to cooperate with each other and chaos reigns. In this scenario, the parts (husband and wife) take on more importance than the whole, which is not what marriage should be about.

To put it more directly, what happens when the parts are so mismatched that they cannot cooperate with each other? Grafting (as I referenced in chapter 4) illustrates the workings of marriage perfectly in the sense that a scion (the fruit-bearing part of one tree plant) is fused together with a rootstock (the part of another tree plant responsible for nutrition) so that both parts, over the process of time, become one plant. This process, which, as I explained earlier, entails the scion and rootstock making a connection of their vascular tissues, can occur between different plant species of the same genus and, sometimes, across genera. Even though grafting plants of different genera is usually less successful, there are cases where this is possible. However, it is outright impossible to graft plant species of different families for the simple reason that plants within a given family share no compatibility with plant species from other families. They have no part with each other. An attempt to graft, say mango with avocado, is an attempt in futility. What part has a believer with an unbeliever? None.

The biblical story of Peter and a sorcerer named Simon answers the question from the standpoint of identity. Peter, infuriated by the sorcerer's offer of money to purchase the gift of the Holy Spirit so that he, too, like the apostles, might lay hands on others, said, *"Your money perish with you, because you thought that the gift of God could be purchased with money! You have neither part nor portion in this matter, for your heart is not right in the sight of God"* (Acts 8:20–21).

What Peter meant was that Simon could not identify with the apostles in the matter of laying on of hands, the same way Paul questions what identity the unbeliever has with a believer in the matter of marriage.

What agreement has the temple of God with idols?

Generally, to be valid and enforceable, contracts must be signed by agreeing parties. This is the idea this question presumes. The Christian—or temple of God, in this instance—can have no binding spiritual contract with his or her unbelieving spouse. This underlying fact that, in the spirit, their marriage is a mere gentleman's agreement with zero significance, dovetails into Paul's writings in 1 Corinthians 7 where he says:

> *Now to the married I command, yet not I but the Lord: A wife is not to depart from her husband. But even if she does depart, let her remain unmarried or be reconciled to her husband. And a husband is not to divorce his wife.*
>
> *But to the rest I, not the Lord, say: If any brother has a wife who does not believe, and she is willing to live with him, let him not divorce her. And a woman who has a husband who does not*

> *believe, if he is willing to live with her, let her not divorce him. For the unbelieving husband is sanctified by the wife, and the unbelieving wife is sanctified by the husband; otherwise your children would be unclean, but now they are holy. But if the unbeliever departs, let him depart; a brother or a sister is not under bondage in such cases. But God has called us to peace.*
>
> (1 Corinthians 7:10–15)

This position does not contradict the lifelong idea of marriage that Jesus presents all through the gospel. Rather, it clarifies it. The rules that apply to Christians in marriage do not apply to unbelievers in the context of the Bible.

Saying that there can be no agreement between the temple of God and idols is another way of affirming that all human beings are one of two beings. They are either spiritual houses for God, where His occupancy signifies a form of exclusion, or self-absorbed ideologues limited by their lack of appreciation for a divine being. This affirmation is anchored on the extant idea of two natures that are never in accord with each other—the first being the nature of God that dominates the Christian and then the nature of man in his fallen state without Christ. It is to be accepted in principle that there can be no spiritual accord between the two so that marriage between a believer and a nonbeliever is completely carnal, bearing little or no spiritual meaning to God and portending dire consequences of heartache, sorrow, and pain. Remember, God has called us to peace, which means oneness with each other—a husband with his wife. Nevertheless, there can be no peace in a marriage of the temple of God with idols.

From the five follow-up questions that Paul asks on unequal yoking, it is easy to conclude that, like Christianity, marriage is supernatural. The Christian is directly referred to as righteousness, light, Christ, a believer, and the temple of God. Marriage requires participation, commonality, vocal harmony, identification, and endorsement in a strictly spiritual sense, and these questions all point to the fact that marriage is, indeed, supernatural.

"There is a deliberate reason why God caused Adam to fall into deep slumber before He created Eve—so that at every point of conflict in marriage, man will turn to God," one of my friends, Ohonmi Ehonwa, would aptly say. It is instructive to note that neither Adam nor Eve were aware when God made a decision to marry them. It is apparent that God originated marriage to lead human beings back to Him, which is why making the decision on whom to marry should never be offhand. It should be God-led every step of the way.

> *Which of you by worrying can add one cubit to his stature? So why do you worry about clothing? Consider the lilies of the field, how they grow: they neither toil nor spin; and yet I say to you that even Solomon in all his glory was not arrayed like one of these. Now if God so clothes the grass of the field, which today is, and tomorrow is thrown into the oven, will He not much more clothe you, O you of little faith? Therefore do not worry, saying, "What shall we eat?" or "What shall we drink?" or "What shall we wear?" For after all these things the Gentiles seek. For your heavenly Father knows that you need all these things. But seek first the kingdom of God and His righteousness, and all these things shall be added to you.* (Matthew 6:27–33).

Chapter 7

The Compatibility Question

If you have gotten to this point, you must understand by now that the success or failure of any marriage depends on how a husband and wife mutually view marriage. What I refer to as the state of marriage—whether it be a codependent relationship, a partnership, or a union—is often determined by the composite understanding of the husband and wife, taking into account their backgrounds, mindsets, and experiences with respect to marriage.

The Pair of Us

We can distill the lessons of earlier chapters into one idea that every husband and wife ought to have: marriage is a "we" or "us" relationship and not a "you and I" relationship. The individualism of being single must give way to the collectivism of marriage, failing which all kinds of marital problems spring up. What God has joined, let not man put asunder—including the joined; this is a divine injunction that cares very little about that much-thrown-around word in today's culture: compatibility.

My eighth year in marriage was the most difficult. I had gradually morphed into a resentful person, largely because I hated my job at that time, coupled with the fact that I had racked up nearly $40,000 in debt, trying to impress people who really did not care. As would be expected, my wife and I fell headlong into daily squabbles about money, about working late, and just about everything. I would often take off on long walks when our fights heated up, to prevent them from degenerating into fisticuffs. Those walks gave me time to think and often pray about the turbulence of that period. I would honestly reflect on my roles in aggravating my wife while recounting some of my own injuries to God.

"Where did I go wrong, Lord?" or "Oh Lord, help me" were the first words I would gasp, counting one step in front of the other, as soon as I was out the house. In moments, I would get answers, floating up to my conscious mind, on how I might behave and respond better toward my wife in the future. "Two things you have absolutely no control over are the past and your spouse," wafted up into my mind on one of my post-fight strolls. In fact, most of the things I share in this book I learnt over many nightly walks back in 2013. Nevertheless, "Marriage is a 'we' or 'us' relationship and not a 'you and I' relationship" made the most impact, as I hope it will for you by the time you finish reading this book. The icy mass that was my pride, selfishness, and opaqueness, where my wife was concerned, began to thaw from that day up until now, so much so that I honestly do not know whether I would still be married had I not encountered those words.

Compatibility Is a Myth

Another phrase that helped anchor me during that period of my life centered on compatibility. No two human beings are, by themselves, compatible. What many assume to be compatibility is a myth. Pheromones (a chemical factor secreted to trigger social responses in members of the same species) and oxytocin (a hormone that acts as a neurotransmitter in the brain and is responsible for social interaction) are largely responsible for what many consider compatibility or the lack of it. More often than not, the decline in pheromones and/or oxytocin levels in people is the silent problem expressed in the awful phrase *irreconcilable differences*. As Russian writer Leo Tolstoy posits,

"What counts in making a happy marriage is not so much how compatible you are but how you deal with incompatibility."

Compatibility is a work of God.

> *Then the rib which the Lord God had taken from man He made into a woman, and He brought her to the man. And Adam said: "This is now bone of my bones and flesh of my flesh; she shall be called Woman, because she was taken out of Man."* (Genesis 2:22–23)

This delineates the roles of God, husband, and wife, and the hierarchy without which things fall apart. A man or woman may choose any spouse they desire—with or without the input of the Holy Spirit—but God bears the sole charge of joining both of them in holy matrimony, according to Matthew 19:6.

This is why Christians seeking divorce on grounds of incompatibility grieve God. What God has joined, no man may separate. To the married in Christ, God made you and your spouse compatible with each other when you married. You are no longer two but one. If God makes the husband and wife compatible at the onset of their marriage, how then does a Christian man or a woman, seeking divorce, cite irreconcilable differences?

"In the beginning, God created the heavens and the earth," the Bible says in Genesis 1:1. By the second verse, the earth had become formless and empty with darkness enveloping its entire watery surface. Then bit by bit, God calls forth light, the atmosphere, vegetation, and animals before creating human beings. All through the story, it appears that God is in the habit of unraveling things ex nihilo. However, this supposition diminishes at the first words that God speaks: "Let there be light" or "Light be," according to the transliterated Hebrew. Light did not come out of nothing; it must have existed somewhere between Genesis 1:1 and Genesis 1:2. This is the same principle that carries over into almost everything God created, including marriage. God joined Adam and Eve but left the unraveling of it to the man.

"And Adam said: "This is now bone of my bones and flesh of my flesh; she shall be called Woman, because she was taken out of Man."

God wrought compatibility. "They are no longer two but one." Nevertheless, God bequeaths the unearthing of this compatibility to the couple through the headship of the man. Much like God called light out of darkness, the husband must recognize and unravel the oneness that already exists between him and his wife. To do so, he must take God's side. He must acknowledge that, indeed, he and his wife are one and that there could be no secrets kept from or competition with his spouse and vice versa. Spouses who keep secrets from each other or compete with each other simply have not yet gotten the memo. Their oneness remains buried under the debris of selfishness, and the buck unequivocally stops at the husband's table.

If a marriage's thermometer is the wife, its thermostat is the husband. "*The husband is the head of the wife as Christ is the head of the church.*" Nineteenth century French sociologist Emile Durkheim borrowed the word *anomie* from French philosopher and poet Jean-Marie Guyau to explain the social (and not the personal) causes of suicide in his 1897 book, *Suicide*. Durkheim disagreed with general view of that day, which sought to explain that the causes of suicide were purely personal, enmeshed in a person's string of ill luck, followed by depression. He argued that a rapid change of the standards and values of a society took its toll on individuals, predisposing them to feelings of disillusionment and nihilism before which some of them, unable to cope, committed suicide.

Though Durkheim's arguments acknowledge personal and social factors in suicides, they do not acknowledge the degree to which these factors relate with each other up until the point where an individual takes his or her own life.

The structure of marriage is similar in that the husband and wife are one in the eyes of God. Hence, to divorce is, in a sense, a form of suicide with the personal factors playing a more significant role than the social factors. Without debate, the perspective a couple has about marriage will underlie the state of their marriage. This is where the injunction, "What God has joined, let not man put asunder" (in Matthew 19:6) holds sway. Here, it is implicit that the mere thought of divorcing one's spouse is sin. We miss the mark when we mentally take apart what God put together. Certainly, this is the first step toward the ever-present suicides of marriages in contemporary Christian culture.

Abdication of Gender Responsibilities

The other personal factor contributory to the disintegration of marriages is the abdication of gender responsibilities that the Bible so amply prescribes. *"Do not be conformed to this world, but be transformed by the renewing of your mind, that you may prove what is that good and acceptable and perfect will of God"* (Romans 12: 2).

Contrary to the general view that submission is a wife's domain alone, the husband is asked to submit in all his interactions with God and his wife if marriage is to be as heaven desires. The scriptures charge the husband to dwell with his wife according to knowledge and treat her with consideration as the delicate part of the union (see 1 Peter 3:7). Now if that is not submission, I wonder what is. For a man to dwell with his wife according to knowledge, he must have a keen interest in studying her. You cannot study someone to whom you do not submit.

Then, the husband is required to treat his wife as his delicate part—this being the actual meaning of the term *weaker vessel*—giving to her the honor due her so that their prayers are not hindered. He is to love her as his own self, regarding her views as his own, and, at the least, negotiating the views he does not agree with in the spirit of love. The apostle Paul delivers an anecdote in his first letter to the Corinthians that ties in well with the delicate nature of the wife to her husband and, by extension, their union. He writes:

> *If the whole body were an eye, where would be the hearing? If the whole were hearing, where would be the smelling? But now God has set the members, each one of them, in the body just as He pleased. And if they were all one member, where would the body be? But now indeed there are many members,*

> *yet one body. And the eye cannot say to the hand, "I have no need of you"; nor again the head to the feet, "I have no need of you." No, much rather, those members of the body which seem to be weaker are necessary. And those members of the body which we think to be less honourable, on these we bestow greater honour; and our unpresentable parts have greater modesty, but our presentable parts have no need. But God composed the body, having given greater honour to that part which lacks it, that there should be no schism in the body, but that the members should have the same care for one another.* (1 Corinthians 12:17–25)

Clearly, husband and wife must cooperate as one body under God, but it does not end there. This holy triad—God, man, and wife—must maintain a balance of power that entails the husband's unalloyed submission to God without which his wife may not be able to submit to him and he to her.

> *Husbands, love your wives, just as Christ also loved the church and gave Himself for her, that He might sanctify and cleanse her with the washing of water by the word, that He might present her to Himself a glorious church, not having spot or wrinkle or any such thing, but that she should be holy and without blemish. So husbands ought to love their own wives as their own bodies; he who loves his wife loves himself. For no one ever hated his own flesh, but nourishes and cherishes it, just as the Lord does the church. For we are members of His body, of His flesh and of His bones. "For this reason a man shall leave his father and mother and be joined to his wife, and the two shall become one flesh." This is a great mystery, but I speak concerning Christ and the church. Nevertheless, let each one of you in par-*

ticular so love his own wife as himself, and let the wife see that she respects her husband. (Ephesians 5:25–33)

Largely, the wife may be the thermometer or feeler of a marriage, but her husband is the thermostat. By his submission or lack of it, he determines which of the three states his marriage morphs into at any point in time. Like matter, which can be in gaseous, liquid, or solid state, a marriage can be a codependency, a partnership, or a union. A man's submission to God and his wife, in the proper order, is his tool for bringing the union through the many troubles that those who marry are certain to face in this life (see 1 Corinthians 7:28).

Chapter 8

The State of Codependency

The most common state that marriages are in is the state of codependency. I know this because of the prevalence of abuse in many marriages across the world today. Abuse—whether it be physical, emotional, verbal, or financial—is the number one indicator of a marriage that is in a state of codependency. Another symptom is regret fuelled by resentment. An estimated 50 percent of women across the world regret marrying whom they married, and there is a reason for this. The men they marry are not showing leadership.

In the words of speaker and author, John C. Maxwell, "Everything rises and falls on leadership." Biblically, the husband determines whether the marriage grows or disintegrates. This is why the Jesus message assigns more responsibility to the husband than it does the wife. Though the Bible clearly spells out the roles of husband and wife, many, even in the Church, wrest the scriptures to impose a message of gender imparity between men and women that the Bible does not communicate. Gender struggles and the debates for and or against it have not helped the worldview of marriage. Many men and women have developed a false sense of who a husband is: that somehow, he is his wife's master, overlord, or oppressor. The world's major religious systems and mainstream media have reflected and perpetuated this view, rightly eliciting the outcry against patriarchy. This seriously needs to be corrected. The false sense of the husband being lord and master has been the backbone of codependency in marriages across Christendom.

The prophet Jeremiah prophesized about how God's people have committed two evils (see Jeremiah 2:13). First he says they have abandoned God, the fountain of living waters, and, by extension, His ways. Then he concludes by saying God's people have hewn for themselves broken cisterns that can hold no water. Implicitly, many have abandoned God's original idea about the husband being the head of his wife and adopted a worldly view skewed by gender inequality.

The husband is master—do not get me wrong—but not the way the world looks at it. I hate to burst the bubble in some Christian circles, but Jesus said he that would be lord among you must be your servant (see Matthew 20:25–26). In essence, being a husband entails servanthood and is a more hallowed office than the shallow view we give it in popular culture. First, he is the intermediary between the Lord and his wife. He serves both of them with the gravest of loyalty and love as is prescribed for his office. This office of intermediary between his Lord and his wife is so sacred that if a husband will not submit to God and love his wife, she can find no way to submit to him within the context of the word of God, even if she desires to.

The Portrait of Codependency

A marriage in a codependent state is one in which one or both spouses have persistent feelings of regret, concerning their marriage, based on the actions or personality of their significant other. For want of a better phrase, it is that feeling of wanting to be rid of your spouse at the slightest occasion. More often than not, the result of persistent and deep-seated resentment of one spouse toward the other is that marriages in this state can feel parasitic, the predominant feature being ingratitude. Ingratitude is actually a form of resentment or, at best, a direct consequence of it. We do not appreciate what we resent.

Ingratitude takes a debilitating toll on both spouses in the sense that it is contagious. Anyone—including the spouses involved—can easily detect when a marriage has fallen into the sickness of codependency by listening to the spiteful manner in which conversations are carried on between husband and wife. *"Husbands, love your wives, just as Christ also loved the church and gave Himself for her,"* the Bible admonishes in Ephesians 5:25. The other two qualities of this state of marriage besides resentment are arrogance and deceit, making it an evil triad.

Canadian clinical psychologist Jordan B. Peterson was the first to talk about this evil triad in his postulations about the dangers of postmodernism and its quest to annihilate individualism and free speech. Fundamentally, one could trivialize this as mere ideology, but nothing could be truer and indeed more dangerous to the human family than spouses who have become arrogant, deceitful, and resentful toward each other. One spouse begins to see the other as a liability in some way. It could happen both ways. Maybe he does not earn enough money or even have a job. Alternatively, maybe she is not frugal enough and spends impulsively, bleeding the family into debt. Whatever the case is that has caused the evil triad to exist between you and your spouse, the good news is codependency is mutable once you can view your marriage the Jesus way.

The rule of thumb in problem-solving is to first identify what the problem is. It pays to get a glimpse of what this state of codependency in marriage is using the lenses of God's Word so that it is easily decipherable in your marriage. In addition, and as a quick disclaimer, there is nearly no marriage that will not experience a state of codependency to some degree at one point or the other. What is important is knowing when and how to break your marriage out of the prison that is this state.

God asked Adam how he knew he was naked and whether he had eaten the forbidden fruit. His reply: "It was the woman you gave me." He implicated her and, in a sense, abdicated his responsibility to God. In a moment, the evil triad of arrogance, resentment, and deceit had beclouded Adam's view so that Eve, whom he had once recognized as the bone of his bone and the flesh of his flesh, had now become the emblem of his self-loathing, unbeknownst to him. No man yet hated himself, the Bible says, and yet, Adam, by his actions in the garden that day, showed substantial hatred for himself.

It is self-evident that codependency starts with the self-hatred of the husband to some degree. It suffices to say that the relational toxicity, domestic violence, emotional abuse, verbal abuse, and other forms of abuse experienced in many marriages today are rooted in a man's hatred for himself—and this is not to bash men at all. The Bible says, "No one ever yet hated his own flesh; but nourishes and cherishes it, just as the Lord does the church" (see Ephesians 5:29).

One Bible story of a marriage in the state of codependency is that of Nabal and Abigail.

> *Now there was a man in Maon whose business was in Carmel, and the man was very rich. He had three thousand sheep and a thousand goats. And he was shearing his sheep in Carmel. The name of the man was Nabal, and the name of his wife Abigail. And she was a woman of good understanding and beautiful appearance; but the man was harsh and evil in his doings. He was of the house of Caleb.* (1 Samuel 25:2–3)

Nabal, whose name is translated *folly*, is the archetypal anarchist, a rebel against the order of things. He is the husband so full of himself; he refuses to submit to God and his wife. Abigail, on the other hand, represents the best of women, full of empathy and beauty. She is the best a man can get. Yet, things fall apart.

Nabal's unguarded statements to David's militia (see 1 Samuel 25:5–10) threatened the lives of everyone around him so much that one of his employees had to call upon Abigail to intervene. Nabal's actions in refusing David's request for provender demonstrates his ignorance of the consequences, not just for himself but also for his entire household. Nabal husbands fail to see how their poor choices to remain unemployed, be abusive, or generally refuse to show leadership threaten their own existence and the existence of others. Inadvertently, their wives must clean up their messes after them as Abigail does for Nabal.

Nevertheless, women are not wired to lead but to colead, to confirm direction, not offer it. A good illustration would be a captain and an executive officer of a navy nuclear submarine. The captain's job is to lead the mission while the executive officer's is to keep the captain on task. While the captain is appraised by how successfully the mission is completed, the executive officer or XO, as he or she might be called, must account to the naval central authority for how he or she ensured the captain followed plans and procedures in the completion of their assigned mission, particularly when the mission became difficult to complete. The wife is this executive officer in a marriage, whose assignment and voice must keep her husband on task with respect to their marriage's mission.

Abigail ends up throwing her husband under the bus (in 1 Samuel 25:25–26) to stave off David's wrath and save herself along with the rest of their household. Apparently, this is the same reason wives of Nabal husbands shame them privately and, sometimes, in public.

Nabal's eventual death, after a night of drunken revelry and Abigail's relation of her encounter with David, is metaphorical. Husbands, who refuse to submit to God and the order of things, facilitate the death of their own marriages. A man cannot fix his marriage until he views it as God does.

Even more symbolic is how David marries Abigail after Nabal's demise. David is everything that Nabal is not and more. It can be concluded that, to break a marriage out of the state of codependency, Nabal must die and then David can take his place. David is the archetype of submission to God. He has a good sense for the sacred order of things. David recognizes that he and his wife are a single entity under God.

Unmanned Marriage

Marriage is too important for God to leave without a leader. Just as Christ is the leader of the church, the husband is the leader of the wife and, by extension, the marriage. Together, they lead their family, society, and the world.

Nevertheless, some husbands refuse to be men in their marriages, and this is the source of codependency. God's mandate in Ephesians 5:25 is a mandate to men to love their wives just as Christ loved the church and gave Himself for her. This is where feminism fails in Christian marriage. It addresses the recriminations of male domination by following it into the same ditch, and none is the better for it. Male domination in a marriage is a form of blindness as to what marriage is. "If the blind lead the blind, both of them wind up in a ditch," Jesus says (see Luke 6:39).

In truth, marriage calls the husband to manhood and not maleness. Religion and culture may subsume the male in a patriarchal way of thinking but not the Christian man. In his heart, the Christian man is bound to love like Christ. The Greek word translated *husbands* in Ephesians 5:25 ("Husbands love your wives") actually means "men." Anyone can tell apart a male from a man by the way he treats his wife. The male may have a problem with taking advice or direction from his wife, but a man loves her enough to consider her view, particularly if she has the superior argument. The male may refuse to get a job to support his family for many reasons, but a man loves his wife too much to put her through that sort of pain. The male may see a weaker gender in his wife, but a man sees the part of himself without which he is incomplete.

I remember where I was on the day the first autonomous car hit and killed a pedestrian because I, too, was in my car on the road that day. The news filtered in through the car stereo that an autonomous car, operated by Uber, had struck and killed a woman, causing the ride-sharing company to halt trialling its autonomous taxis. Elaine Herzberg, forty-nine, was walking across a four-lane road with her bicycle in Tempe, Arizona, when the headlights of a self-driving SUV flashed at her, knocking her over without a moment's notice. The bigger twist to the story was that the car, although in autonomous mode, had a safety driver behind the wheel whose eyes were off the road. Her colleagues' investigation calculated that had Rafaela Vasquez's eyes been on the road, she would have been able to stop more than forty feet before impact.

Codependent marriages bear a striking resemblance to the cause of that accident. Like that SUV, driving at about forty miles per hour, unmanned marriages bring about avoidable casualties.

What Unmanned Really Means

Marriages do not need males; they need men. "The husband is the head of the wife as Christ is the head of the church" (see Ephesians 5:23). This is indisputable when you understand the context of headship the Bible presents. Headship is not about male domination. It is about being the fountainhead of love in a marriage just as Jesus is the fountainhead of love in Christianity. When the wife submits, she submits to the unconditional love that her husband gives based on his submission to the love of God in Christ Jesus. The husband, who does not understand the biblical meaning of his headship, confines himself to the religious and cultural expectations of his gender.

Every religious and cultural system approaches marriage from the standpoint of gender—absolve the man and shame the woman. This is the same standpoint that Adam took after the fall when he said, "The woman whom you gave to be with me, she gave me of the tree, and I ate" (see Genesis 3:12). In her husband's mind, Eve was to blame for the fall, and he promptly indicted her. This remains true today for every man whose marriage has slipped into codependency.

The daughters of Eve are not also exempt from bad behavior in codependency. In codependent marriages, they become rebellious to male domination as a way of preserving themselves. After all, God did not create her to submit to domination but to the part of her that effuses unconditional love. In large part, feminism in marriage derives its vigor from the husband, who is more gender-driven than manhood-driven. "*Husbands* [translated from the Greek word *andreas*, which means "men"], *love your wives as Christ loved the church and gave himself for her*" is a testament to the Christian man's capacity to love his wife enough to get a job, look away from other women, inspire his children, live a godly life, and even die for his wife.

If you are a husband reading these words, God wants you to man up. By this, I mean you need to man your marriage. You are not the chauvinistic overlord that the world tries so hard to label you. Rather, you are the fountainhead of pure love to your wife, just as Christ is the fountainhead of love to the church. If you will not submit to Christ's love, neither can she to your love. Remember that by Bible standards, a husband is not a man until he loves his wife the same way Christ loves the church and gave Himself for her. When a husband does otherwise, he leaves his marriage unmanned, and this is what the state of co-dependency is.

From Codependency to Infidelity

Of the three different states a marriage can be in, people caught in the state of codependency are the ones most predisposed to having affairs. The number two rule in the infidelity playbook is making the person you want to have an affair with sense the inadequacy you feel in your spouse—rule number one being lust.

Putting one's spouse down behind their backs in the presence of someone of the opposite sex points to dissatisfaction in the relationship. It can also help diagnose the state of a marriage. No matter how minute, a snide remark about your spouse should alert you to something you hate about yourself; otherwise, you could end up sabotaging your marriage. Whether it is flirting with a coworker, watching pornography, chatting with someone on social media, or actually sleeping with someone who is not your spouse, infidelity entails secrecy. Such behavior counters the Jesus idea that the two have become one. There should be no secrets between you and your spouse. The moment you start being secretive toward your spouse, watch it. Your marriage has slipped into codependency in some way. The husband is simply not functioning according to his purpose in marriage—the fountainhead of love. As the heart pumps to ensure the proper circulation of blood to other parts of the body, so the husband pumps love into marriage. Without love, his wife cannot submit to him. She cannot love him or even be completely faithful.

*Husbands, love your wives, just as Christ also
loved the church and gave Himself for her, that He*

might sanctify and cleanse her with the washing of water by the word, that He might present her to Himself a glorious church, not having spot or wrinkle or any such thing, but that she should be holy and without blemish. So husbands ought to love their own wives as their own bodies; he who loves his wife loves himself. For no one ever hated his own flesh, but nourishes and cherishes it, just as the Lord does the church. For we are members of His body, of His flesh and of His bones. "For this reason a man shall leave his father and mother and be joined to his wife, and the two shall become one flesh." This is a great mystery, but I speak concerning Christ and the church. Nevertheless, let each one of you in particular so love his own wife as himself, and let the wife see that she respects her husband. (Ephesians 5:25–33)

If you have ever wondered about a wife's mean-spiritedness or lack of submission when disagreements arise, this is what it comes down to. Her husband failed to supply her with the needed love. Notwithstanding, the wife must see to it that she respects her husband.

Chapter 9

The Partners

"And the Lord said, 'Indeed the people are one and they all have one language, and this is what they begin to do; now nothing that they propose to do will be withheld from them" (Genesis 11:6).

Partners trade with each other. They trade their weaknesses for strength, the resources they have for the ones they do not have or for the ones they want. The whole idea of partnership is to collaborate in such a way that we can surmount obstacles or attain goals that may be exclusively or mutually beneficial to the collaborating parties.

Using Genesis 11:6 as a point of reference, the people were one, and when they were, nothing would be impossible to them. Then they decided to use their oneness to oppose God by building the Tower of Babel. So God decided to split them up by giving them different languages so that they could neither understand one another nor conspire against God anymore. To survive from here on meant they had to become partners, shifting their energies from single pursuits to the exchange of ideas and meaning.

As I write this chapter, the central bank in my home country, the Central Bank of Nigeria, has just entered into a bilateral agreement to swap currencies with its Chinese counterpart, the People's Bank of China. The agreement, intent on boosting trade between the two countries, will see 720 billion Nigerian naira exchanged with sixteen billion Chinese yuan in goods and services. Many marriages today are like bilateral partnerships, merely providing a platform for the exchange of resources toward the sole purpose of dealing with challenges characteristic of daily living. Many people marry their allies, even though it is never the plan at the outset. And after a couple of years—having pursued careers, put their children through school, paid off the mortgage, and surmounted many other challenges—they split up.

Why? Why do couples, having lived together for twenty to thirty or even forty years, split up?

Because they never knew, let alone changed, the state of their marriages. They were allies all the while they were together, engaging in sexual activity and sharing common battlefronts, including childcare, utilities, housing, and all. As they grew older, they conquered these fronts one by one until there were no more fronts to conquer. Caught, as it were, in a state of peace, nearing the end of their lives, bearing the scars of battle and never really knowing each other, the alliance disbands.

It is the same for young people in this state of marriage. The moment the partnership marriage loses sight of a common enemy, it collapses.

Somewhere between the '80s and the '90s, the term *partners* became popular for describing couples in all kinds of relationships. It checked all the boxes: convenient, gender-neutral, all-encompassing, and, most of all, politically correct. Nevertheless, while this term rightly pluralizes general relationships between people, it has done more harm to marriages, given the peculiarity that the Jesus message notes:

"*They* [husband and wife] *are no longer two but one—and what God has joined together, let no one separate*" (Matthew 19:6).

Many times, all through the epistles, Christians are admonished not to think or talk like the rest of the world. We are mandated not to be conformed to the world but to be transformed through the renewing of our minds (see Romans 12:2). Nothing defies the Lord Jesus on the subject of marriage as the phrase *my partner*, used in reference to a husband or wife. Yet contemporary culture has socialized many Christians to think and talk this way.

Referring to your spouse as your partner presents a problem because by doing so, you mentally and vocally separate what God has joined. Marriage is not an *I-thou* relationship as acclaimed psychologists Harville Hendrix and Helen LaKelly Hunt propose in their highly praised book, *Getting the Love You Want*. The *I-thou* dynamic suggests that husband and wife are two separate individuals, seeking to achieve or retain their connectedness to each other. This is counter-scripture. Your spouse is not your partner but a part of you. What the Jesus message proposes marriage to be has been watered down by the very idea of being partners. Call it semantics if you want, but being part of another is not the same thing as being partners with another. The latter is the root of the rising divorce rates while the former calls for self-acceptance, self-responsibility, and self-change.

When a man and a woman marry, they become a new self. Self-acceptance means that both spouses accept each other wholeheartedly. Self-responsibility means they take ownership of shortcomings while leveraging strengths. Self-change means that they work together for growth.

Marriages in the partnership state are characterized by personal agendas, selfishness, and competition. Husband and wife, who should be components of each other, talk and work as individuals, limiting their contribution to the bare minimum. You hear things like "my money," "my car," "my children," "my life," "your choice," or "your car" in benign conversations between husband and wife. These kinds of conversations also occur when the marriage slips into a codependent state, but they are never under friendly circumstances.

The sad part of the partnership state is that this is the best-case scenario for marriage in the world today. Mainstream media has done a great job of socializing couples to see themselves as partners instead of parts of each other. Though marrying with a partnership mindset has its merits in the sense that couples can hold themselves to some level of accountability and expect things from each other, it leaves a back exit. In their minds they are two, not one, and, therefore, dissoluble at the slightest whiff of discord.

It is not a surprise that irreconcilable differences are the most cited reason for divorce in our day. Many marry and divorce like they put on and take off a jacket when, in actuality, the process is more like having a vital organ transplant and then taking it out again. Like marriages in the state of codependency, the ones that remain in the partnership state are disposed to divorce simply because both states do not agree with the Jesus message. Both states separate what God has joined, first from the mindsets of the couple and then along with other ramifications, ranging from finances to parenting style. Male domination and female subservience are also characteristic of the partnership state as they are of codependent marriages. Since both of these states do not agree with the Jesus view of marriage, they are no doubt products of the fall.

Genesis 3:16 states, *"To the woman He said: 'I will greatly multiply your sorrow and your conception; in pain you shall bring forth children; your desire shall be for your husband, and he shall rule over you.'"*

By this, we understand the origins of the power dynamic in marriage states that do not conform to the Jesus message. The wife, desiring her husband, would seem like what every man dreams of until you realize what it really means. In such instances, the wife directs her desires, good or bad, at her husband so that the same way she can make him feel like superman is exactly how she can also emasculate him—her tool being her tongue. With her tongue, the wife manipulates her husband, praising and shaming, when necessary, as a coping technique until such a time when her husband submits himself to God's design and begins supplying agape to their marriage.

On the other hand, the husband is an autocrat who bears rule over his wife once their marriage slips into the codependent or partnership state. He is less than the man he should be in Christ's context because of the Fall. The fall—and its many consequences—is what a Christian man yields to when he does not yield to the words of Jesus: "not two but one."

This is why feminism and male domination have no place in the Christian marriage. For the very fact that husband and wife are not partners but parts of each other, we are all mandated to see them as one indivisible person. All chaos in marriage stems from not grasping this reality.

"Therefore what God has joined together, let not man separate" (Mark 10:9).

Not a Covenant but a Sacrament

Contrary to what you have heard, marriage is not a covenant. It is a sacrament. For the very reason that a covenant entails two or more parties, entering into an agreement for a specific purpose, it is not in accordance with the Jesus definition of marriage. In the Bible, God entered several covenants with the children of Israel for the sole purpose of establishing commitment. The children of Israel were required to do their part so that He could do His part. It was through these covenants that God was able to bless humanity after the fall of Adam in the garden. It was standard practice for kings in the old days to enter into covenants for trade and military purposes. Today, we call these covenants trade agreements and treaties.

Sacraments, on the other hand, are an outward showing of the most fundamental truths of Christianity. Their essence unravels some of the mysteries of Christ with simple activities. For example, baptism carries weightier meaning. Baptism presupposes the baptized person's identification with the substitutionary work of Jesus Christ in dying and resurrecting from the dead. In other words, it is the outward showing of that individual's acceptance of Jesus's death, burial, and resurrection on his or her behalf. It is a notification to the world that the old sinful creature has died and a new creation has been born. This is what it means to be born again. You believe and then you are baptized (see Mark 16:16).

Marriage is like this too. When Christians marry, it signifies the oneness of Christ and His church. This is what Paul alluded to in Ephesians 5:32 when he said, "I speak of Christ and the Church." You cannot understand Christianity if you do not understand the truth about marriage, neither can one grasp marriage without first understanding what Christianity entails. Christians are not partners with the Lord but members of His body, of His flesh, and of His bones (see Ephesians 5:30). Marriage is, therefore, symbolic of three things that the Christian shares with Christ:

- A self-identity
- A commonwealth
- A destiny

A Self-identity with Christ

Self-identity is self-concept. It is the estimation of oneself as distinguished from others. "Who am I?" asks the typical person, struggling with his or her own identity. This question presumes a fixed answer. It also takes, as fact, the derivation of identity from one's preconception of self, juxtaposed with the preconception of others. The Christian's identity is shrouded in Christ. Ample portions of the New Testament project Christians as one with the Lord Jesus so much that it is futile to attempt to divorce Christians from Jesus. Even non-Christians are quick to call out Christians who err in one way or the other for behavior that goes against the grain of who they consider Jesus to be. This is the idea that marriage also entails. Husband and wife are not two individuals but one individual. Just as a Christian is one with Jesus, husbands and wives are one. This alone should pause any competition and strife between husband and wife.

Jesus had a remarkable understanding of His identity. We know this by the contents of His prayer documented in John 17:20–23:

> *I do not pray for these alone, but also for those who will believe in Me through their word; that they all may be one, as You, Father, are in Me, and I in You; that they also may be one in Us, that the world may believe that You sent Me. And the glory which You gave Me I have given them, that they may be one just as We are one: I in them, and You in Me; that they may be made perfect in one, and that the world may know that You have sent Me, and have loved them as You have loved Me.*

Pronouns have stirred up all kinds of debates in contemporary culture for the very fact that identity is never amorphous at any point in time. As at the time of this writing, the University of Minnesota, Minneapolis was considering a pronoun policy to curb indignities suffered by transgender or gender nonconforming students known as misgendering—when a person is called by a name or personal pronoun they no longer accept. The whole furor in support of the right of the individual to choose their personal pronouns fails in logic on the premise that pronouns—apart from the first person singular—are not personal. This also supposes that biology has no say in whom society deems male or female. Nevertheless, identity is both endogenous and exogenous. To posit that it stems only from the endogenous—and then jettison the biology of the person for his or her psychological preferences—rationalizes mindlessness.

In His prayer for His believers, the church, Jesus uses the appropriate pronoun *we* to elaborate the *you-in-me–I-in-them* relationship that Christ or, more aptly, Christianity entails.

Paul, the apostle, echoes Jesus in the portion of his letter to the Colossian church where he writes:

"*Set your mind on things above, not on things on the earth. For you died, and your life is hidden with Christ in God. When Christ who is our life appears, then you also will appear with Him in glory*" (Colossians 3:2–5).

Marriage mirrors this intimate relationship so that the most appropriate pronoun by which spouses can identify themselves is not "you and I" but "we." When a man and a woman are engaged (and by this I mean—in a committed relationship exclusive of sex), their identities are separate. However, the moment they have sex, they collapse their identities into each other and take on an entirely new identity.

Baptism also communicates this truth. Everyone that believes and is baptized collapses their old identity in Christ and takes on an entirely new identity. This new identity, the Christian in Christ in God, is what Mark 16:15–18 articulates:

> *Go into all the world and preach the gospel to every creature. He who believes and is baptized will be saved; but he who does not believe will be condemned. And these signs will follow those who believe: In My name they will cast out demons; they will speak with new tongues; they will take up serpents; and if they drink anything deadly, it will by no means hurt them; they will lay hands on the sick, and they will recover.*

Identity implies function. This is why identity determines functionality or dysfunctionality in a myriad of contexts. An adult female who identifies as an agender (a person without a gender) will be less likely to get pregnant or even function as a mother. The other side of the coin is demonstrated when the seven sons of Sceva, itinerant exorcists, attempted to function like Christians in casting the demons out of a demon-possessed man. They said, "*We exorcise you by the Jesus whom Paul preaches*" (see Acts 19:11–20).

Before overpowering, wounding, and stripping all seven of them, the demoniac said to them, "*Jesus I know, and Paul I know; but who are you?*"

The sons of Sceva lacked the identity to use the name of Jesus and, therefore, could not function as He would have. The apostle John cements this idea of the Christian's shared identity with Jesus with the words, "*Love has been perfected among us in this: that we may have boldness in the day of judgment; because as He is, so are we in this world*" (1 John 4:17).

The husband and wife must identify as parts of each other and not partners; otherwise, they will malfunction, breeding the kind of chaos that makes it possible for Satan to overpower, wound, and strip Christian families of their God-ordained purposes on earth.

A Commonwealth with Christ

Christian marriages mirror the commonwealth of Christ. We are sufficient in Him just as He is sufficient in us. This is what Paul alludes to when he writes, *"The Spirit Himself bears witness with our spirit that we are children of God, and if children, then heirs—heirs of God and joint heirs with Christ, if indeed we suffer with Him, that we may also be glorified together"* (Romans 8:16–17).

Our shared identity with Jesus as God's children grants us unhindered access into the commonwealth of God. We are not coheirs as some translations suggest; we are joint heirs with joint access. Jesus cannot disburse heaven's wealth on earth without the Christian, and the Christian cannot disburse it without Jesus. It is apparent that, for any divine intervention to occur in the affairs of men, a prior agreement must exist between Jesus and a Christian or group of Christians, which is actually the whole import of prayer.

In the same light, husband and wife are sufficient in each other in terms of access to mutual resources. This is not just financial, even though money serves as a powerful example for illustrating the concept of commonwealth.

The signing rules of the traditional joint account constrain the signatories to the account to operate it jointly. Anybody may deposit funds into the account, but to access the funds, all parties must agree. This pooling together of resources and the agreement by all involved parties on how to utilize them underpins Christianity and marriage. The entire New Testament supports the fact that the Christian can only access this divine commonwealth by agreeing with Jesus, the Word of God.

Romans 10: 9–10 reads thus, *"That if you* CONFESS *with your mouth the Lord Jesus and believe in your heart that God has raised Him from the dead, you will be saved. For with the heart one believes unto righteousness, and with the mouth* CONFESSION *is made unto salvation."*

The words *confess* and *confession*, translated from the Greek root word *homologia*, actually means "to speak in consent." Essentially, the Christian's access into the commonwealth is his vocalized identification with the Jesus message. This is also true of marriage. It means that husband and wife must agree that they jointly own and administer all resources in their marriage—be they spiritual, financial, intellectual, or emotional. It means that every dollar, counsel, experience, perception, spiritual encounter, and so on belong to the both of them jointly. It does not matter whom God spoke to; the information belongs to them, and they must agree on its usage. Husband and wife are heirs together of the grace of life (see 1 Peter 3:7) and must consider this with respect to their commonwealth. Often, I have encountered wives who say, "My money is my money, but my husband's money is our money." This thought contravenes scripture in the same way that deeming personal assets and liabilities of each spouse as separate does. For example, if your spouse had racked up a debt before or during the course of the marriage, both of you now bear the responsibility for that debt. It also means that if your spouse got a job at Apple or wherever, you both bear the responsibility for ensuring high performance on that job. There can be no competition in a marriage. To compete with your spouse in any form presumes that you see him or her as a partner and not a part of you. This counters the Word of God.

A Common Destiny

Like Jesus Christ and His church, husband and wife share a common destiny, no matter the ramification.

> *Now He who searches the hearts knows what the mind of the Spirit is, because He makes intercession for the saints according to the will of God. And we know that all things work together for good to those who love God, to those who are the called according to His purpose.* FOR WHOM HE FOREKNEW, HE ALSO PREDESTINED TO BE CONFORMED TO THE IMAGE OF HIS SON, THAT HE MIGHT BE THE FIRSTBORN AMONG MANY BRETHREN. *Moreover, whom He predestined, these He also called; whom He called, these He also justified; and*

whom He justified, these He also glorified. (Romans 8:27–30)

In Christ, our destiny is to fit the image of God's Son. What does this mean? The word translated *Son* from the Greek word *Huiou* implies reaching a maturation point in character without which the child of God cannot manifest complete dominion over evil in this world. Paul writes of how the entire creation waits eagerly for Christians to reach this maturation point (see Romans 8:19). Imagine that God has placed in us the ability to divert earthquakes, cure cancer, and exert authority against the corruption of this world, but many of us are not there because many of us have not reached our destiny.

Jesus reached this place of destiny by His absolute obedience to God. Twice in the Gospel of Matthew, we read:

"And suddenly a voice came from heaven, saying, 'This is my beloved Son, in whom I am well pleased'" (Matthew 3:17).

"While he was still speaking, behold, a bright cloud overshadowed them; and suddenly a voice came out of the cloud, saying, 'This is my beloved Son, in whom I am well pleased. Hear Him!'" (Matthew 17:5).

On both occasions, Jesus is referred to as God's Son, not necessarily in terms of being God's offspring but in terms of the maturation of His person into the destiny of dominion that God had preplanned. The Bible shows clear demarcation between Jesus's sonship by nativity and His sonship by destiny (Luke 1:32). The former is an act of God while the latter is an act of Jesus's obedience. This is why Jesus's attainment of the status of Son (Huiou) is so pleasing to God. Just like Jesus, the church must attain this destiny of sonship. It is God's stated expectation of us, and we do well to please Him by living up to it. For more details on this, check out my book titled *Destiny*.

Every marriage has one destiny. This is why who you marry is so important. Many have taken the position that husband and wife have separate destinies or that the wife's is somehow subordinated to that of her husband. For the umpteenth time, husband and wife are one person in the eyes of God. When God told Abraham, "In your seed shall all the nations be blessed," He was also speaking to his wife, Sarah.

Just as Christ is the head of the church, the husband is the head of the wife. Apart from being the fountainhead of God's love to his wife, the husband, like Jesus Christ, must understand and model their God-given destiny to his wife. The destiny of every marriage is both generic and specific. Generically, God desires to raise godly children out of every marriage. Specifically, God may desire you and your spouse to lead a local church and risk your lives for the gospel, like Priscilla and Aquila. Whatever the Lord has called the husband to do, he calls the wife to do too and vice versa.

Remember, God authors no confusion. Husbands or wives, who work at cross-purposes with each other for whatever reason, need to sit back to reexamine their motives.

The partnership state is a product of worldly thinking. This thinking also underpins the idea that marriage is a covenant. Marriage is not a covenant but a sacrament—a depiction of Jesus Christ and the church, a reflection of the image of God. The two become one in such a way that acting or even thinking of husband and wife as though they are separate individuals clearly contradicts God and calls for repentance.

Chapter 10

The Union

When life squeezes you, it is what is inside you that is going to come out. This is why husbands need to be drinking constantly from the fountain of everlasting love through constant fellowship with the Word of God. The union state of marriage happens when husband and wife align with God in thoughts, words, and actions, concerning their oneness. Here, they think as they are—one indivisible unit under God. In Bible pictographs, the husband is the head while the wife is the body.

"So husbands ought to love their own wives as their own bodies; he who loves his wife loves himself" (Ephesians 5:28).

If a human body is to function properly, there can be no competition between the head and the body. This simple idea is what husbands must achieve with their wives.

Just as Jesus Christ loves His body, the church, so must the husband love his wife. Just as Jesus is the exemplar of divine sonship (as explained in the previous chapter), the husband must exemplify godliness and a spiritual sense of destiny to his wife.

Having a union state of mind is the grand old secret of marriage. As American country musician Jimmy Dean once said, "Nobody, man or woman, has ever wrecked a good marriage." The fundamental understanding that marriage is a "we interplay and not a "you and I" arrangement is what makes a good marriage. As earlier stated, this understanding must emanate from the husband. As Jesus is one with the church, the husband must be one with his wife. He must take ownership for their union such that all that happens in his wife's life actually happens to *them*. Only then is his wife able to reciprocate. Remember, the husband's function is twofold: he provides headship (according to Ephesians 5:23), and then, he provides unconditional love (according to Ephesians 5:25). These two, he must get by, first, submitting to the headship and unconditional love of Jesus Christ before passing them on to his wife.

I find that some husbands and wives prioritize their relatives or children before their spouses. This is wrong and, at the least, a subtle form of self-hatred that needs to be checked. Jesus leaves us without doubt as to God's love matrix by which every human being should live.

Popularized as the Great Commandment and recorded in all the synoptic gospels, Jesus said:

> *"You shall love the Lord your God with all your heart, with all your soul, and with all your mind." This is the first and great commandment. And the second is like it: "You shall love your neighbour as yourself." On these two commandments hang all the Law and the Prophets.* (See Matthew 22:35–40, Mark 12:28–31, and Luke 10:25–28)

The entire schema from Jesus's categorizations of first and second commandments makes it easy to conclude that obedience to the latter commandment is consequent upon obedience to the former. In other words, love for God must precede love for oneself, and only then can a person express love to others. You simply cannot love others until you have learned to love yourself, and you cannot truly love yourself until you have first loved God. God first, yourself next, and others last.

As I have stated earlier, when two people marry, they become a new self. Therefore, prioritizing your children or relatives over your spouse is not just foolish—it reeks of self-hatred. In fact, every treatment meted to one's spouse apart from love borders on self-hatred.

You cannot think union and cheat on your spouse, divert the family's financial resources, or not maintain full disclosure about practically everything. Being in the state of union means that you buy into God's idea of marriage as absolute oneness with your spouse. It also means that you and your spouse will be able to actualize God's overriding pursuit for marriage, which is to populate the world with godly people.

"But did He not make them one, having a remnant of the Spirit? And why one? He seeks godly offspring. Therefore, take heed to your spirit, and let none deal treacherously with the wife of his youth" (Malachi 2:15).

This aside, thinking union as a married person means that you are able to reap the day-to-day benefits that God embeds in every marriage.

Money

From a monetary point of view, being in a state of union means financial transparency and probity. It means that every dime earned by the union stays in the union. In other words, you and your spouse jointly and transparently make decisions about your investments, savings, expenditures, and charitable donations.

According to a recent survey of marriages in America conducted by Ramsey Solutions, a leading company in financial education owned by foremost finance author and talk show host, Dave Ramsey, "Money fights are the second leading cause of divorce, behind infidelity."

The survey went on to include the following findings:

- Nearly two-thirds of all marriages start in debt. Forty-three percent of couples married more than twenty-five years started off in debt, while 86 percent of couples married five years or less started off in the red—twice the number of their older counterparts.

- One-third of people, who say they argued with their spouse about money, say they hid a purchase from their spouse because they knew their partner would not approve.
- Ninety-four percent of respondents, who say they have a great marriage, discuss their money dreams with their spouse, compared to only 45 percent of respondents, who say their marriage is okay or in crisis. Eighty-seven percent of respondents, who say their marriage is great, also say they and their spouse work together to set long-term goals for their money.
- Sixty-three percent of those with $50,000 or more in debt feel anxious about talking about their personal finances. Almost half (47 percent) of respondents with consumer debt say their level of debt creates stress and anxiety.

Imagine how practicing complete transparency renders these money problems completely powerless to ruin your marriage. More than this, maintaining complete transparency with your spouse plugs the money leakages or, at least, gives proper account for the leakages. It also helps with better financial planning.

Parenting

Nothing creates a safer space for raising children than parents in the union and the state of their marriage. As aforementioned, God's overriding purpose for marriage is to populate the earth with godly people. However, in no other state of marriage is this achievable. In the state of codependency, the husband is an anarchist, like Nabal, and in the state of partnership, he is a contributor. Maternal instincts, which are a constant because of the bond shared by mother and child, are simply not enough to raise children into godly adults. The absence of a father predisposes a child to all kinds of evil, but his presence can equally do great harm as long as it does not conform to the Jesus message of "the two become one."

The anarchist in a codependent marriage abuses not only his wife but also his children in a way that makes them a liability to society. When a man is not submissive to God's love, he cannot love anyone. He is the source of society's worst ills. His wife, on the other hand, becomes a revolutionary and, sadly, may approach her parenting as she does her husband. She must battle to prevent her resentment toward him from spilling into her relationship with her children. She may be successful, or she may not. Whatever the case is, the state of codependency is bad for parenting.

The contributor in a partnership is like this as well. Since he and his wife function as partners, he has his own approach to raising children while she has hers. Children under these kinds of parents are more likely to be manipulative if they realize that both parents communicate different agendas or that they do not communicate the same values. This schism in marriage produces multiple personality types in children. This is the case of the seven-year-old who, having been denied permission by her mom to go out and play with friends, goes to her father for permission behind her mom's back and gets it. When her mom confronts her for flouting her instruction, the little girl's defense is, "Daddy let me go." In her mind, both parents are co-parents with equal powers to grant her desire and are, therefore, exploitable, whereas this should not be the case. Biblical parenting is joint parenting and not coparenting.

"Did He not make them {husband and wife} one, having a remnant of the Spirit? And why one? He seeks godly offspring. So take heed to your spirit that you do not deal treacherously" (Malachi 2:15 Modern English Version).

The state of union is the only state in which a marriage can fulfill God's desire for godly offspring. Husband and wife must agree at all times before they reach any decision and their children must understand this consensus, particularly when making requests. They must understand that no is no and yes is yes from a consensus perspective between both parents.

Psychologists have said that the sociopath is a creation of his or her environment. This is true. Parents with the wrong mindsets about marriage inadvertently fail to raise godly children because of their inability to create the needed environment.

Who is the sociopath by the way? The sociopath grows out of the child who never learned to practice self-restraint before his or her conscience began to function fully. Over time, as the child learned to violate his or her budding conscience, growing into adulthood, the child dulled the sense of right and wrong to the point of no return. The child, now a man or woman, would have succumbed to so many unruly passions for which he or she is unable to assume responsibility, even now that he or she is an adult. This is bad. The union state of marriage on its own impels a sequence of righteousness such that parents are well equipped to cater for the spiritual, emotional, and psychological well-being of their children.

Legacy

God's plans for every family are always transgenerational. God is not the God of Abraham, Isaac, and Jacob for nothing. Continuity and succession matter a lot to Him such that His blessings last a thousand generations while His wrath extends to the third and fourth generations, according to the Bible. The genealogy of Jesus is a detailed record of how forty-two generations conspire in one way or the other to bring about the Messiah's birth, death, burial, resurrection, and everything accomplished thereby.

The union state of marriage is the only facilitator for passing God's intentions from one generation to another. As earlier mentioned, the husband in the union state is a conduit of divine direction and unconditional love to his wife. Then, husband and wife jointly pass direction and love to their children.

> *And these words which I command you today shall be in your heart. You shall teach them diligently to your children, and shall talk of them when you sit in your house, when you walk by the way, when you lie down, and when you rise up. You shall bind them as a sign on your hand, and they shall be as frontlets between your eyes. You shall write them*

on the doorposts of your house and on your gates.
(Deuteronomy 6:6–9)

The union state of marriage is the only effective way to attain financial transparency, be great parents to your children, and leave them a legacy of riches and righteousness. It is the only way to raise godly offspring.

Let us look at Malachi 2:15 one last time:

"But did He not make them one, having a remnant of the Spirit? And why one? He seeks godly offspring. Therefore, take heed to your spirit, and let none deal treacherously with the wife of his youth."

There is a way to be married, and this entails being union-minded. If you operate as codependents or partners, you are dealing treacherously, and we now know who God will hold responsible for this. Nevertheless, it is not enough to know how to be married; you must also understand why. The sexualization of society has made many people think that marriage is for sex. This is not the case. God seeks to populate the earth with people all right, but He seeks to populate it with godly people. He seeks people who will solve problems, bring order to all the climatic chaos, and pattern the earth after heaven. He seeks transgenerational legacies.

People are God's most valuable creation, and only the Christian marriage in a state of union can deliver the quality of people that God wants.

God's desire for godly people remains in tandem with His first instructions to Adam and Eve in the Garden of Eden. He told them to "*be fruitful and multiply; fill the earth and subdue it; have dominion over the fish of the sea, over the birds of the air, and over every living thing that moves on the earth*" (Genesis 1:28).

Paul writes of how the whole of creation waits for the revealing of the sons of God (see Romans 8:19). This is exactly what the state of union will produce as we make the decision to reposition our marriages to agree with Jesus.

Chapter 11

Repositioning Your Marriage

Repositioning your marriage presupposes that your marriage is not in a good place. It could mean that your marriage is either in the state of codependency or partnership. By now, you should have realized that the state of any marriage is actually a reflection of inner thoughts, mindsets, or beliefs about marriage.

The moment you change your inner beliefs about marriage, your marriage will change. This is what the prophet Malachi meant when he said, "Therefore, take heed to your spirit, and let none deal treacherously with the wife of his youth" (Malachi 2:15). Transforming your marriage means that you and your spouse have a sit-down, peer into each other's eyes, and accept the truth that you are part of each other. No prayer or fasting will do this for you, just an acceptance of the truth.

Next, you both have to come clean about how your wrong thinking allowed you to hurt each other and then forgive each other. All hurt in marriage stems from the false assumption that you and your spouse are partners and not parts of each other.

> *Husbands, love your wives, just as Christ also loved the church and gave Himself for her, that He might sanctify and cleanse her with the washing of water by the word, that He might present her to*

Himself a glorious church, not having spot or wrinkle or any such thing, but that she should be holy and without blemish. So HUSBANDS OUGHT TO LOVE THEIR OWN WIVES AS THEIR OWN BODIES; HE WHO LOVES HIS WIFE LOVES HIMSELF. FOR NO ONE EVER HATED HIS OWN FLESH, BUT NOURISHES AND CHERISHES IT, *just as the Lord does the church.* (Ephesians 5:25–29)

No one hurts himself or herself, at least not knowingly. This is why coming to the agreement that both of you are one person allows you to forgive each other.

Going forward, your new beliefs must form the basis for your thoughts, words, and actions. "We are one" forms the basis for how you pray, handle finances, parent, and do every other thing.

The husband supplies divine direction and unconditional love to the union based on his submission to the Lord Jesus Christ, while the wife confirms the divine direction and unconditional love of her husband by her submission to him.

Whether your marriage is in the state of codependency or partnership right now, what is ideal is that you both realize what Jesus meant when He said, "Not two but one" in Matthew 19:6.

There is supernatural peace on the other side once you accept the oneness that already exists between you and your spouse. The marital issues between the two of you simply dissipate.

Chapter 12

Looking Unto Jesus

The story of Peter and Jesus walking on water is very symbolic in the sense that even though countless sermons on faith have found root in it, what the story actually talks about is undiluted focus. According to the account of the apostle Matthew, Jesus constrained His disciples to go ahead of Him to the other side of the Sea of Galilee so that He could disperse a crowd they had miraculously fed and join them later. After the crowd had dispersed, Jesus went up a mountain to pray, and when evening came, He was all by Himself in this secluded place. Meanwhile, the boat carrying the disciples had encountered rough weather at sea such that contrary winds hindered their journey. Then at about three o'clock in the morning in the thick darkness, the disciples made out a figure coming toward their boat, walking on the sea. They were troubled. "It must be a ghost," some of the disciples cried out of fear.

"Calm down, people, it is me. There is no need to be afraid," Jesus said.

It was then that Peter spoke up. "Lord, if it is you, ask me to come to you on the water," he said.

"Come," Jesus replied.

Immediately, Peter got out of the boat and headed toward the master. This is the same kind of enthusiasm found among intending couples and newlyweds, but then, the euphoria wears off. Peter's homoeostasis kicked in, and he began to observe the waves again. They billowed boisterously, and in that brief moment, Peter lost focus of Jesus. He began to sink. Then he returned his focus to the master and cried out, "Lord, save me."

Jesus immediately stretched out his hand, grabbed him, and said, "O you of little faith, why did you doubt?"

The story ends when both of them get back into the boat and, immediately, the wind ceases.

The chief moral of this story is not faith but focus. Like Peter, the Christian in the midst of adversity is imperiled by what he or she chooses to focus on.

Apostle Paul writes:

> *Therefore we also, since we are surrounded by so great a cloud of witnesses, let us lay aside every weight, and the sin which so easily ensnares us, and let us run with endurance the race that is set before us, looking unto Jesus, the author and finisher of our faith, who for the joy that was set before Him endured the cross, despising the shame, and has sat down at the right hand of the throne of God.* (Hebrews 12:1–2)

Our focus must be on Jesus in the storms of marriage. This is how you lay aside unbelief and run the course of your marriage with the required stamina. The original Greek phrase translated *looking unto Jesus* actually means to look away from something else and focus on Jesus. In the midst of marital difficulties, we must look away from the other definitions we have of marriage and settle on how Jesus defines marriage, using His words as a firm foothold. The story of Peter and Jesus walking on water aptly supports this. Peter looked away from Jesus and began to sink. He returned his focus, looked again at Jesus, and actually completed a walk back into the boat, on water.

In a certain sense, looking unto Jesus is motivational. Motivation is very important in every aspect of human behavior. Whatever you do, be it dieting, working out, or studying the Bible, motivation plays an important role in regard to starting and finishing the activity. Jesus is the author and finisher of our faith or, more precisely, the motivator of every action in our daily life—since the just live by faith (see Romans 1:17, Galatians 3:14, and Hebrews 10:38). This means that Jesus must motivate every action or activity in the Christian marriage from beginning to end.

What I have not said up until this point in this book is that there will be storms in your marriage, no matter the state it is in. The union state is not conflict-proof. In fact, all that the state of union does, in regard to conflict, is to fortify marriage against implosion. Your marriage will, however, face loads of external aggression. Man's days are full of trouble, and as Apostle Paul notes, *"Even if you do marry, you have not sinned. Nevertheless, such will have trouble in the flesh, but I would spare you"* (1 Corinthians 7:28).

The presence of Jesus in the day-to-day doings of marriage is threefold. Jesus is the Word of God, the love of God, and the Spirit of God (see John 1:14, Titus 3:3–5, and 2 Corinthians 3:17). As we see in the story of Peter and Jesus walking on the sea, the moral of it is that husband and wife must walk as one, looking unto Jesus to thrive amidst the storms of life.

Looking Unto the Word

The Word of God is the composite of divine knowledge. Apostle John writes, *"And the Word became flesh and dwelt among us, and we beheld His glory, the glory as of the only begotten of the Father, full of grace and truth"* (John 1:14).

The composite of divine knowledge became a man called Christ, who eventually transcended the confines of His physical body and became an ecosystem of believers. *Christ*, by definition, is the sum of Jesus and every person—living or deceased—who has professed His lordship through water baptism. John notes that as Jesus is, so are we in this world (see 1 John 4:17).

The Christian—husband or wife—is the Word of God that became flesh. Just as any creature bears oneness with its natural habitat, the Christian bears semblance to the Word of God.

Peter writes:

> *Since you have purified your souls in obeying the truth through the Spirit in sincere love of the brethren, love one another fervently with a pure heart, having been born again, not of corruptible seed but incorruptible, through the word of God which lives and abides forever.* (1 Peter 1:22–23)

Paul corroborates:

> *You are our epistle written in our hearts, known and read by all men; clearly you are an epistle of Christ, ministered by us, written not with ink but by the Spirit of the living God, not on tablets of stone but on tablets of flesh, that is, of the heart. And we have such trust through Christ toward God. Not that we are sufficient of ourselves to think of anything as being from ourselves, but our sufficiency is from God, who also made us sufficient as ministers of the new covenant, not of the letter but of the Spirit; for the letter kills, but the Spirit gives life. But if the ministry of death, written and engraved on stones, was glorious, so that the children of Israel could not look steadily at the face of Moses because of the glory of his countenance, which glory was passing away, how will the ministry of the Spirit not be more glorious?* (2 Corinthians 3:3–8)

The fabric of the Christian husband and wife is the Word of God, such that it is actually difficult to distinguish both.

"But what does it say? "The word is near you, in your mouth and in your heart" (that is, the word of faith which we preach)" (Romans 10:8).

When you and your spouse have an argument, look unto the Word of God near you and speak it forth. When the bills show up and threaten the sanctity of your home, look unto the Word of God and speak it forth. Also, recognize that the Word of God in you may not always require you to speak. Sometimes, it may require you to do something, like getting a new job or calling your spouse on the phone to say pleasant things. It may also require you to keep your mouth shut when tempers are running high. Whatever it is, the Word of God will call on you to do something.

Like Peter, if you act based on the problem, you will be overcome by it. However, if you look unto the Word of God and do what He says to you, you will go through any situation.

> *No temptation has overtaken you except such as is common to man; but God is faithful, who will not allow you to be tempted beyond what you are able, but with the temptation will also make the way of escape, that you may be able to bear it.* (1 Corinthians 10:13)

The way of escape out of every trial, tribulation, or temptation is the Word of God. If you hear God's Word today, yield yourself to Him.

Looking Unto Love

Like the Word of God, the love of God weaves into the spiritual makeup of the Christian. Romans 5:5 tells us that God has broadcast His love over our hearts like a plane broadcasts fertilizer over a farm acreage. The love of God is the true estimation of your worth. Looking unto love means that one focuses on the true worth of a being and nothing else as a basis for interaction.

"For God so loved the world that He gave His only begotten Son, that whoever believes in Him should not perish but have everlasting life" (John 3:16).

God's estimation of humankind was not just Jesus but sonship. The highest value that God places on all humanity is the worth of His Son.

As mentioned in the last chapter, God's love matrix—love God, love yourself, and love others—follows a definite sequence because true worth emanates from God. You cannot estimate yourself properly until you have estimated God by His own estimation of Himself. *"We love Him because He first loved us"* (1 John 4:19). Only after we have estimated ourselves properly can we truly estimate others.

Looking unto love implies action. God is love, and love is a verb. As William Paul Young puts it in his wildly successful book *the Shack*, "God is a verb." Just like God, we are verbs. The next time you and your spouse enter into a hurtful situation, look unto love. Let God's estimation of your husband or wife guide you. Remember that your spouse is you, and no man ever yet hated his own flesh but nourishes and cherishes it, just as the Lord does the church (see Ephesians 5:29).

Looking Unto the Holy Spirit

Looking unto Jesus also entails looking to the Holy Spirit. The Holy Spirit is to a Christian what Jesus was to His disciples before He died and rose again: a teacher and a guide.

Of the Holy Spirit, Jesus said to His disciples,

> *These things I have spoken to you while being present with you. But the Helper, the Holy Spirit, whom the Father will send in My name, He will teach you all things, and bring to your remembrance all things that I said to you.* (John 14:26)

The Holy Spirit is a present helper in the midst of befuddling circumstances, particularly in your marriage. Jesus said He (the

Holy Spirit) would teach the Christian all things. This includes the Christian man and woman bound together in matrimony. Again, looking unto the Holy Spirit indicates action on the part of the believer. It means fellowshipping with Him.

> *Now in the church that was at Antioch there were certain prophets and teachers: Barnabas, Simeon who was called Niger, Lucius of Cyrene, Manaen who had been brought up with Herod the tetrarch, and Saul. As they ministered to the Lord and fasted, the Holy Spirit said, "Now separate to Me Barnabas and Saul for the work to which I have called them." (Acts 13:2)*

How did He speak? He spoke through one of them during the meeting, just as He will speak through you or your spouse as you take time to fast and minister to Him.

Paul writes:

> *The wife does not have authority over her own body, but the husband does. Likewise, the husband does not have authority over his own body, but the wife does. Do not deprive one another except with consent for a time, that you may give yourselves to fasting and prayer; and come together again so that Satan does not tempt you because of your lack of self-control. (1 Corinthians 7:4–5)*

Paul's admonition to the married in 1 Corinthians 7:4–5 takes for granted that couples agree upon specific periods of time for fellowship with the Holy Spirit. You and your spouse may pray together every day, and this is in order. However, looking unto the Holy Spirit may mean looking away from your phones, food, or outside company for a specific amount of time to pray, fast, and study the Bible. You and your spouse will have times when, like Peter, you will need the Lord speaking expressly to you on what next to do. At points where life's journey bifurcates or there is a challenge you need to overcome, the union will have to look unto Jesus in the person of the Holy Spirit.

Make sure you and your spouse know how to receive instructions from the Holy Spirit. The Holy Spirit speaks to the Christian through four channels:

- The inward witness (Proverbs 20:27, 1 Corinthians 2:9–10)
- The gift of prophecy (1 Corinthians 14:4–5)
- The gift of interpretation of tongues (1 Corinthians 14:27)
- Visions (Acts 16:9–10)

While I would love to elaborate on how the Holy Spirit speaks to Christians, I have listed them in order of frequency—the inward witness being the most frequent way He speaks and visions being the least.

Looking unto Jesus in your marriage means that you and your spouse act in tandem with the Word of God, the love of God, and the Spirit of God, not just when matters arise but also on a day-to-day basis. This is the state of union at its perfection. There truly is nothing like it.

Chapter 13

The Question of Submission

Today's husband has a false sense of lordship, and it is because he has yet to understand submission. "I am the man of the house." Many men would assert to suggest the absolutism of the husband-father archetype in the home. However, this idea is not from God but from the devil. In fact, the concept of submission has been the thin demarcating line between the kingdom of God and the domain of darkness, even before God created Adam and Eve.

> *How you are fallen from heaven, O Lucifer, son of the morning! How you are cut down to the ground, you who weakened the nations! For you have said in your heart, "I will ascend into heaven, I will exalt my throne above the stars of God; I will also sit on the mount of the congregation on the farthest sides of the north; I will ascend above the heights of the clouds, I will be like the Most High." Yet you shall be brought down to Sheol, to the lowest depths of the Pit. Those who see you will gaze at you, and consider you, saying: "Is this the man who made the earth tremble, who shook kingdoms, who made the world as a wilderness and destroyed its*

cities, who did not open the house of his prisoners?" (Isaiah 14:12–17)

The usurpation of authority has always been Satan's plan. Cain killing his brother, Abel, the attempt at building the Tower of Babel, and Saul's choice to keep spoils from the capture of the Amalekites against divine instruction—all bear the trademark of the chief conspirator. The outcomes are the same. Things fall apart, the center cannot hold, mere anarchy is loosed upon the world. Cain becomes a hobo, the Mesopotamians become so confused linguistically that they abandon the tower, and Saul loses his kingship (see Genesis 4:8–12, Genesis 11:1–9, 1 Samuel 15: 5–21).

This is what many of today's husbands are—usurpers of divine authority. Like every other thing that bears Satan's imprint, such men toy with the collapse of their homes by touting their supposed dominion.

"But the husband is the head of the wife, even as Christ is the head of the Church," some would say. Literally, this is correct but not in the context of hierarchy or importance.

Since his fallout with God, Satan has sought dominion over human beings for the sole purpose of mocking his creator. If he (the devil) could not ascend above the Most High, he might as well ascend above the image of God if they let him. This is why the very facet of human existence outside Christ is hierarchical in nature.

> *Then the devil, taking Him up on a high mountain, showed Him all the kingdoms of the world in a moment of time. And the devil said to Him, "All this authority I will give You, and their glory; for this has been delivered to me, and I give it to whomever I wish. Therefore, if you will worship before me, all will be yours." And Jesus answered and said to him, "Get behind Me, Satan! For it is written, 'You shall worship the Lord your God, and Him only you shall serve.'"* (Luke 4:5–8)

Satan, the god of this world, fashioned the systems of this world to allow him to dominate men through other men in every sphere from religion to literature to technology. For thousands of generations, the acceptance of hierarchy has characterized human societies. "The hand of the strong bear rule" aptly gives credence to Darwin's theory of natural selection. However, humankind is not innately hierarchical but communal and collaborative. After all, human beings are made in the image and likeness of a collaborative God.

Jesus said:

> *The kings of the Gentiles exercise lordship over them, and those who exercise authority over them are called 'benefactors.' But not so among you; on the contrary, he who is greatest among you, let him be as the younger, and he who governs as he who serves.* (Luke 22:22–26)

The unbelieving husband is, by socialization, an overlord but not the Christian husband. To truly honor God, to possess all that He planned, and to experience and enjoy all that God has for his children in marriage—everything depends on the Christian couple renewing their minds with the Word of God. The Christian husband is a servant. He serves God and his wife in constant communion with the two of them.

> *Husbands, love your wives, just as Christ also loved the church and gave Himself for her, that He might sanctify and cleanse her with the washing of water by the word, that He might present her to Himself a glorious church, not having spot or wrinkle or any such thing, but that she should be holy and without blemish. So husbands ought to love their own wives as their own bodies; he who loves his wife loves himself. For no one ever hated his own flesh, but nourishes and cherishes it, just as the Lord does the church. For we are members of His body, of*

> *His flesh and of His bones. 'For this reason a man shall leave his father and mother and be joined to his wife, and the two shall become one flesh.' This is a great mystery, but I speak concerning Christ and the church. Nevertheless let each one of you in particular so love his own wife as himself, and let the wife see that she respects her husband.* (Ephesians 5:25–33)

Christian men who dominate their wives do so citing this portion of the Bible, forgetting that the husband must submit twice before ever his wife submits to him. "Husband, love your wife" is both an admonition and a prerequisite for God to bless your marriage. By loving his wife, the husband submits to God. Second, by loving her, he submits to his true self—the union.

> *I beseech you therefore, brethren, by the mercies of God, that you present your bodies a living sacrifice, holy, acceptable to God, which is your reasonable service. And do not be conformed to this world, but be transformed by the renewing of your mind, that you may prove what is that good and acceptable and perfect will of God. For I say, through the grace given to me, to everyone who is among you, not to think of himself more highly than he ought to think, but to think soberly, as God has dealt to each one a measure of faith.* (Romans 12:1–3)

The domination some men try to exert over their wives is born out of pride—that satanic implant in every culture, religion, or social construct that touts the superiority of men over other men or, in this case, husband over wife. The husband thinks of himself more highly than he ought to think. Unaware that this way of thinking gives ample room for Satan to take over and dictate the course of marriages and failing to renew their minds, many Christian men perpetuate a lie. The husband is one with his wife and not superior to her.

"God resists the proud and gives grace to the humble." (See Proverbs 3:34, James 4:6, 1 Peter 5:5.)

Humility is submission to God. It is accepting divine placement in the schema of God's creation. God places the husband side by side his wife as a single entity. The husband who ascends above his wife is like Satan attempting to ascend above the Most High. He will meet resistance and disgrace from God.

"For this reason a man shall leave his father and mother and be joined to his wife, and the two shall become one flesh'; so then they are no longer two, but one flesh. Therefore what God has joined together, let not man separate" (Mark 10:7–9).

Marriages will remain dysfunctional until men understand Mark 10:7–9 and allow it to renew their thinking.

Until husbands are manly enough to submit to the Word of God, wives will never fully submit to them.

The Submitted Wife

While the husband is the head of the wife and the part of her that supplies divine love and order, the wife affirms her husband's love by her submission (or, as is the case with unbelievers, repudiates his lack of love by not submitting to him).

Nothing excuses the Christian wife from submitting to her husband—except his requests of her contravene the scripture.

> *Wives, submit to your own husbands, as to the Lord. For the husband is head of the wife, as also Christ is head of the church; and He is the Saviour of the body. Therefore, just as the church is subject to Christ, so let the wives be to their own husbands in everything.* (Ephesians 5:22–24)

This does not mean women submit to men as to the Lord. In fact, accusations of the Bible, being a sexist book based on scriptures like the one above, actually flounder when we look at the contexts of these scriptures.

Ephesians 5:22 says, "Wives, submit to your own husbands." It does not say, "Wives, submit to every husband" but "to your own husbands." Moreover, it gives a premise for why wives should submit to their husbands in verse 23. It says, *"For the husband is head of the wife, as also Christ is head of the church; and He is the Saviour of the body."*

In other words, the wife submits to her own husband because he is her head, just as Christ is the head of the church and the savior of the body. The original Greek word for *head* used all throughout the New Testament in the context of how husbands relate to their wives is the word *kephale* from which we derived words like *cephalic* and *cephalad*. It means "head," as it pertains to an organism and not as it pertains to a social construct. In essence, the husband is the head of the wife exactly the way the head of a lion relates to the rest of his body. Alternatively, this same lion may be the head of his pride, comprising other lions, lionesses, and cubs.

In the context of body parts, this means that, as the lion's body submits naturally to the direction of its head, even so the wife submits to the direction of her husband. The eyes, ears, nose, and mouth are in the head, which, aside from providing sensory functions of sight, hearing, smell, and taste, also provide balance for the body. I cannot say this enough, but husband and wife are not the social construct that sociologists presume; they are parts of each other, and without coherence, they cannot achieve anything.

Paul writes, *"Wives, submit to your own husbands, as is fitting in the Lord"* (Colossians 3:18).

Natural order and not domination is why wives submit to their husbands. Each part has its roles in the fulfillment of God's predetermined destiny for the marriage union. A marriage where husband and wife fail in their roles to each other is a recipe for chaos, which is why the Bible says in Ephesians 5:18–21:

> *And do not be drunk with wine, in which is dissipation; but be filled with the Spirit, speaking to one another in psalms and hymns and spiritual songs, singing and making melody in your heart to*

the Lord, giving thanks always for all things to God the Father in the name of our Lord Jesus Christ, submitting to one another in the fear of God.

If, for any reason, a Christian woman is in a marriage with a non-Christian man, she is not exempted from submitting to her husband in the contexts of their oneness, even though he may see their marriage differently.

The apostle Peter writes, "*Wives, likewise, be submissive to your own husbands, that even if some do not obey the word, they, without a word, may be won by the conduct of their wives*" (1 Peter 3:1).

Submission is what many marriages lack today. When a man submits to God, he creates a sense of safety for his wife by being the Lord's conduit of love and order. When a wife submits, she affirms God's love and order, even if her husband is not a Christian.

Ending this chapter, I would like you to think of two people wearing a horse costume in which one of them is dressed as the head and the forelegs, while the other stoops to form the trunk of the horse and the hind legs. Even though both of them are covered, only the person in front can see through the holes burrowed in the head part of the costume. The other person must depend on the eyes of the person in front for direction and balance, if their movement is to be successful.

Chapter 14

Seventy Times Seven

Being married is one of our God-given opportunities to practice the life we received from God when we came to Christ. We received a life of love, and this has nothing to do with semantics. We are, by nature, love children of a loving God. What He is capable of loving, we also are.

Jesus said, *"By this all will know that you are my disciples, if you have love for one another"* (John 13:35).

As I mentioned afore, love is a verb—meaning, it requires effort. Love is also a decision—meaning, it is intentional. It is not enough for the Christian to possess the nature of love; he or she must decide to put in an effort at loving.

> *Jesus said to him, "You shall love the Lord your God with all your heart, with all your soul, and with all your mind." This is the first and great commandment. And the second is like it: "You shall love your neighbour as yourself." On these two commandments hang all the Law and the Prophets.* (Matthew 22:37–40)

This means husband and wife become intentional about loving God, themselves, and others. If God sees husband and wife as one, it means that the love matrix for a couple starts with their mutual love for God and then their mutual love for each other before they can truly love others.

Until husbands and wives unlearn seeing themselves as separate entities, they cannot love God and others right. In essence, if I do not love God, I cannot truly appreciate His nature of being three persons in one divine being. And if I cannot appreciate this truth, then it will be difficult to see, let alone practice, a similar oneness with a spouse. Let me briefly iterate that love is about appreciation and not possession. If love is actually the truthful estimation of a person, place, or ideal, then Christian husbands and wives cannot truly estimate themselves and others until they have a truthful estimation of God.

> *Then God said, "Let Us make man in Our image, according to Our likeness; let them have dominion over the fish of the sea, over the birds of the air, and over the cattle, over all the earth and over every creeping thing that creeps on the earth." So God created man in His own image; in the image of God He created him; male and female He created them.* (Genesis 1:26–27)

The scripture above gives us a truthful estimation of God in the following sequence:

1. God is collaborative. He said, "Let Us."
2. God has an image and a likeness.
3. God created the human being in His image and likeness.
4. God gave the human being dominion over the animal class and not over other human beings.
5. God's complete image is both male and female. This is the reason He created man and woman.

Love Forgives

If the marriage relationship is the image of God, then it truly matters how spouses love each other as a reflection of how much they love God.

> *Love is patient, love is kind. It does not envy, it does not boast, it is not proud. It does not dishonor others, it is not self-seeking, it is not easily angered, it keeps no record of wrongs. Love does not delight in evil but rejoices with the truth. It always protects, always trusts, always hopes, always perseveres.* (1 Corinthians 13:4–7 NIV)

One of the things the scripture above does not expressly spell out but fittingly infers is that love forgives. It does not keep account of wrongs because love subsumes evil.

Apostle Peter corroborates, *"And above all things have fervent love for one another, for 'love will cover a multitude of sins"* (1 Peter 4:8).

Your spouse is not another but yourself. How are you going to cover the sins of others if you hold a grudge against yourself? How are you going to profess love for God if you cannot forgive yourself?

Apostle Paul writes, *"Brethren, do not be children in understanding; however, in malice be babes, but in understanding be mature"* (1 Corinthians 14:20).

Maturity of understanding means agreeing with God that you and your spouse are one. It means overlooking and covering his or her faults with love. Married people, who refuse to apply forgiveness to their spouses, cannot apply it to any other person. Sometimes, this is why we have vengeful people charge up public spaces with their unforgiving venom. They reflect what is happening to them inside outwardly. Coming to terms with who your spouse is to you, according to the Jesus message, will influence how you esteem yourself and others.

> Then Peter came to Him and said, "Lord, how often shall my brother sin against me, and I forgive him? Up to seven times?" Jesus said to him, "I do not say to you, up to seven times, but up to seventy times seven." (Matthew 18:21–22)

Human beings are not perfect. This is the idea Jesus communicates in His conversation with Peter. If you can count up to four hundred and ninety wrongs done to you, did you really forgive the four hundred and eighty-nine times before?

Forgiveness That Forgets

There is a Christian way to forgive, and this way forgets. First Corinthians 13:5 (NIV) describes love thus: "*It* [love] *does not dishonour others, it is not self-seeking, it is not easily angered,* IT KEEPS NO RECORD OF WRONGS."

If there are any diaries of malicious circumstances anywhere around you, love wants you to burn them up today. If they are social media posts, love requires you take them down. If there are incidents etched in your mind, love requires you turn them over to God.

There is no middle ground between love and hate. You either love your spouse, which is actually self-love, or you hate him or her, which is impossible for Christians, even though some try.

"*Be angry, and do not sin: do not let the sun go down on your wrath*" (Ephesians 4:26).

The Christian couple do not only have to emulate God because they are His children but more so because they are His image. Ephesians 4:26 suggests that we be like God, whose steadfast love never ceases, whose mercies never end but are renewed every morning with great faithfulness (see Lamentations 3:22–23).

Letting a fight or argument go on for more than moments hurts the union in ways that make even God grieve.

> *And this is the second thing you do: You cover the altar of the Lord with tears, with weeping and crying, so He does not regard the offering anymore, nor receive it with goodwill from your hands. Yet you say, "For what reason?" Because the Lord has been witness between you and the wife of your youth, with whom you have dealt treacherously, yet she is your companion and your wife by covenant. But did He not make them one, having a remnant of the Spirit? And why one? He seeks godly offspring. Therefore, take heed to your spirit, and let none deal treacherously with the wife of his youth.* (Malachi 2:13–15)

We may lie to others without many consequences, but lying to ourselves in the context of marriage, repressing the hurts and thoughts of animosity that we may feel toward a spouse, trap us in a bottle of devastation. This is the case when husbands and wives refuse to accept ownership of each other in a marriage.

After all, Paul writes:

> *Let the husband render to his wife the affection due her, and likewise also the wife to her husband. The wife does not have authority over her own body, but the husband does. And likewise the husband does not have authority over his own body, but the wife does.* (1 Corinthians 7:3–4)

We often infer sex in the above scripture, but the proper rendering is obligation. Let the husband render to his wife the obligation due her and, likewise, the wife to her husband. The obligations that husbands and wives have toward each other go beyond sex. They are obligated to treat each other as one entity, and this entails the supply of companionship, fidelity, and forgiveness.

Chapter 15

The Mutuality of Everything

The mutuality of everything is the self-evident rationale behind marriage. It is also the reason why many men and women choose to dissociate themselves from the idea of getting married. Marriage is sharing. The thought of getting married carries with it the sometimes frightening prospect of sharing oneself, one's assets and liabilities, such that it is the reason so many are indecisive about nuptials. You simply must never toy with the idea of marriage if you are not willing to share your life with someone else.

This is what Podkolyosin does in the two-act play *Marriage* by Russian writer Nikolai Gogol. Ivan Podkolyosin, a civil servant, who, like many chronic bachelors, had prevaricated between whether to get married or not, finally decides to contract the services of a matchmaker, Fyokla Ivanovna. Kochkaryov, Ivanovna's aggrieved customer, whom she matched with a difficult spouse, also happens to be friends with Podkolyosin, and supplants her as matchmaker.

Kochkaryov convinces a lovely young woman, Agafya Tikhonovna, whom Ivanovna had initially identified, to choose his friend ahead of three other suitors. Kochkaryov mounts enormous pressure until Agafya and Podkolyosin become engaged. He insists that the wedding take place immediately. Podkolyosin and Agafya begin to dress up, and Podkolyosin enters into a soliloquy about the prospects of marriage. Characteristically, he changes his mind and jumps out the window, leaving his intended unaware of his whereabouts. Everyone looks for Podkolyosin and eventually learn that he has escaped through the window and called a taxi to take him home. Ivanovna returns in the final scene, scolding Kochkaryov for his shoddy matchmaking skills.

Marriage is nothing if it is not about the mutuality of everything between husband and wife.

"*And they were both naked, the man and his wife, and were not ashamed*" (Genesis 2:25).

This is not about both of you liking the same things or about finding things of common interest to you and your spouse. The mutuality of everything in marriage is about compromise. It means that you and your spouse are so transparent and accepting of each other that it enables both of you to make sacrifices for the good of the whole. Transparency and acceptance come down to Christian love, and Christian love comes from loving God.

This is why Luke notes that the early church had all things in common (see Acts 4:32). They let the love of God move them sacrificially. Reaching this point of mutuality is what makes marriages unbreakable. Relationship experts use the phrase *feeling connected* to try to communicate mutuality, but this falls short of God's mind about how spouses are to relate to each other. God does not need you and your spouse to find commonality mechanically through activities both of you enjoy. The truth is there may be none.

You must, at some point in your marriage, own your spouse, and he or she must own you.

An illustrative representation of this concept would be the words of Jesus in John 17:23 where He said, "*I in them, and You in Me; that they may be made perfect in one, and that the world may know that You have sent Me, and have loved them as You have loved Me.*"

This portion of scripture is from Jesus's final prayer for all Christians before He went to the cross. Strikingly, He uses the phrase, "I in them, and You in Me" to communicate the mutuality of oneness with us and the Father. This attests to God's modus operandi from the foundation of the world. Our God communes. In addition, He expects the same interaction from everything that bears His image. This is the mutuality of everything between God and us.

The true intercourse of marriage is not only sexual—you in your spouse and your spouse in you—but spiritual, emotional, financial, and everything else. You must come to terms with your new self. If your spouse has a particular flaw, you must own that flaw because it is now yours. After all, no man ever yet hated his own flesh but nourishes and cherishes it, even as the Lord does the church (see Ephesians 5:29).

Tom Bilyeu of Impact Theory once shared on his podcast an important story about British entrepreneur, Caspar Craven, which, I think, brings home this concept of the mutuality of everything in a marriage.

Caspar and his wife, Nichola, a lawyer, were not happy in their marriage. They had three children, and to top it off, they were struggling to get by financially. One day, the couple decided to create a shared vision statement to try and work out a process for reclaiming their marriage. In doing this, they wrote down all the things each of them was passionate about with a view to identifying areas of overlap. They identified only two, and in that moment, rather than quit based on their differences outnumbering their areas of similarity, they decided to build from the two.

"We started looking not from what was wrong but from what was right," Caspar recounted, "not from what was different but from what was the same."

One of the two things the couple identified was to travel to exotic places and create amazing experiences for themselves and their kids. The Cravens decided to quit their jobs and buy a boat, which took them five years of savings and meticulous planning to pull off. Caspar reminisced that literally writing down a shared vision statement with his wife, dating it five years into the future, hanging it up on the wall in their home, and, eventually, sailing the world for two years with kids transformed who they were as a couple.

In his book about the two-year odyssey titled *Where the Magic Happens: How a Young Family Changed Their Lives and Sailed Around the World*, Caspar writes about a time during their journey when their yacht lost all its power mid-ocean, the nearest piece of land being 500 miles away. Instead of panicking and blaming, they decided to get resourceful about the situation. For the next three days, Caspar and Nichola hand-steered their boat through heavy seas and driving rain until they reached the nearest land, which was Niue, a small island nation in the South Pacific.

"We found humor in the situation, and we worked together as a team," Caspar said. "It became one of our proudest moments, working together."

The Cravens may have been able to break into their mutuality from sailing the world and giving their family an awesome experience, but the Christian couple already have an even greater head start from which to build mutuality—sharing the Word of God with each other and praying together as a single unit on a daily basis. Prayer does this for my wife and me pretty well. We pray as one entity, pouring our soul to God such that no matter who leads the prayer, we are almost fully aware of our desires from God and His desires from us.

Making a conscious effort to learn and know your spouse through and through is fundamental, considering the Jesus message.

"*So then, they are no longer two but one flesh. Therefore what God has joined together, let not man separate*" (Matthew 19:6).

Find a place from where to grow mutuality with your spouse and do not stop until you know him or her like the back of your hand. Understand that you and your spouse are not two but one, and there is only one vision, one mission, and one purpose to your marriage. Your job is to find these.

Chapter 16

Vision and Mission

Every marriage has a vision, a mission, and a purpose. You just have to discover them. Contrary to what many people believe, you do not have to know with exactness what the vision, mission and purpose of your marriage are before you tie the knot.

Some people actually miss it here and, in trying to fix it, divorce their spouses and marry someone else in the hope of fulfilling a dream or vision. You hear things like, '[So and so] and I were not compatible, so we decided to call it quits." This is not to say that the Holy Spirit cannot tell you ahead who to marry. In fact, He does tell Christians who to marry and who to avoid. Some people listen, while others do not. However, who you marry does not change God's purpose for marriage. As Friedrich Nietzsche states, "He who has a why to live can bear almost any how." The vision and mission may vary, depending on who you marry, but God's purpose is always fixed.

Still on Purpose

Another purpose of marriage is that it serves as a blessing receptacle or curse blocker. The Bible calls husband and wife "heirs together of the grace of this life" (see 1 Peter 3:7). This means one spouse can obtain grace for or hinder grace from the other.

It is a fascinating thing, but you have probably come across stories of people, who received a miracle on behalf of their spouses in prayer. God designed marriage such that one spouse could upturn the death of the other. Several testimonies of wives raising their husbands back to life come to mind, but none is as vivid as Linda and David Shublak's testimony.

Tragedy struck when a speeding vehicle struck David, who had gone for an early morning run. Thrown up in the air nearly sixty-five feet, David landed with his head on a hard concrete surface. The doctors gave him up to die as his head began to swell during surgery. Nobody gave David a chance as funeral planning commenced. However, Linda, seeking the Lord's direction on what to do, stumbled upon John 11:25, which was highlighted in her Bible. "I am the resurrection and the life. He who believes in me, even though he die, yet shall he live" was the sign to Linda that David would live again, even though he had been certified brain-dead. Linda kept reading her Bible and praying for her husband, who was on life support despite contrary opinions.

Six days later, David began responding to light. When, in front of the doctors, Linda whispered into his ears to show them that there was life in him, David started moving his legs. The miracle was evident. David Shublak made a full recovery over the next two months, and Jesus was glorified.

The Vision of Your Marriage

A vision is a God-given assignment. It is a broad representation of a God-desired future. Every marriage has one, whether or not you know it. Learning the vision of your marriage is heavily dependent on the ministry of the Holy Spirit.

"However, when He, the Spirit of truth, has come, He will guide you into all truth; for He will not speak on His own authority, but whatever He hears He will speak; and He will tell you things to come" (John 16:13).

The Holy Spirit will guide you into all truth, including the truths about your marriage. When you run into problems, as you definitely will in marriage, the Holy Spirit will be present to counsel you when you reach out to Him.

Jesus said, "*The Helper, the Holy Spirit, whom the Father will send in My name, He will teach you all things, and bring to your remembrance all things that I said to you*" (John 14:26).

In other words, God the Father sends the Holy Spirit in the name of His Son to travel the journey of life with you and your spouse. You have nothing to be afraid of when things seem difficult, if you turn to the Holy Spirit for help.

If this is where you are in your marriage presently, I want you to acknowledge the Holy Spirit right now by saying these words, "Jesus is Lord." Go ahead, say it. "Jesus is Lord."

If you were able to mutter those words, the Bible shows that you did it by the Holy Spirit.

"*Therefore I make known to you that no one speaking by the Spirit of God calls Jesus accursed, and no one can say that Jesus is Lord except by the Holy Spirit*" (1 Corinthians 12:3).

Elements of Vision

A vision from the Holy Spirit, whether it comes to you in words, as it came to Apostle Paul, or in a combination of words and pictures, as it came to most of the Old Testament prophets and Apostle John, must have three elements. It must have:

- an objective
- an activity or activities
- and a tool or a set of tools

The Objective

God's vision for your marriage must have an objective. In Paul's encounter, the objective was for him to take the salvation message to non-Jews (see Acts 26:16–18). In Noah's case, it was for him to salvage his family from an impending flood and repopulate the earth (see Genesis 6:13–18). Whether it was Jeremiah, Ezekiel, or Peter, their visions all had a God-objective behind it. Yours is no different. Do not think that your marriage bears no significance in the grand scheme of things just because the names I have mentioned were all great people in the Bible. God put a vision of having a son before childless and age-stricken Abraham and Sarah (see Genesis 18:1–15) to the end that human beings could become children of God (see Galatians 3:16–18). The objective of God's vision for your marriage will always go beyond you and your spouse. Learn it and cooperate with the Holy Ghost on its accomplishment.

The Activity or Activities

A God-given vision will require participation—an act of faith or several acts of faith. For Paul, it was preaching. Abraham was required to leave his native country to an unknown place, detach himself from his nephew Lot, and sacrifice his son. God's vision for your marriage will necessitate activity in form of a vocation, a detachment from certain people or places, and/or something sacrificial.

"But without faith it is impossible to please Him, for he who comes to God must believe that He is, and that He is a rewarder of those who diligently seek Him" (Hebrews 11:6).

The Holy Spirit will elicit action in the vision statement He gives you for your marriage, just as He did to Priscilla and Aquila, both of whom were tentmakers by occupation (see Acts 18:2–3) but were apostolic workers by divine call (see Acts 18:18, 26).

The activity (or set of activities) involved in the execution of your marriage's God-given assignment is the seed of mutuality. Both of you will have to align as one to accomplish it, and from here, your mutuality will spread to everything else over time.

The Tools or Set of Tools

Our God is faithful. He always equips you with what it takes to accomplish what He wants you to do as a couple. Rest assured, He will put tools or a set of tools inside the vision He gives you. For Paul, it was the gospel of Jesus Christ, the wisdom and power of God. In

Prophet Jeremiah's case, God put His Word in the prophet's mouth (see Jeremiah 1:9–10). Whatever God gives you, use it for the fulfillment of the vision of your marriage.

The Demands of Vision

After you and your spouse have consulted with the Lord and received your vision from Him, write it down. Nothing determines the accomplishment of a goal like writing it down. Some studies show that writing down a goal increases the potential of actualization by up to 42 percent.

> *Then the Lord answered me and said: "Write the vision and make it plain on tablets, that he may run who reads it. For the vision is yet for an appointed time, but at the end it will speak, and it will not lie. Though it tarries, wait for it; because it will surely come, it will not tarry." (Habakkuk 2:2–3)*

You and your spouse need to know and agree upon the vision of the Lord for your marriage. This happens in prayer. From time to time, the Lord will speak to and through both of you, reminding you or prodding you along, so always have a special notepad for each time you and your spouse fellowship with the Lord.

Be assured, God will speak to you both each time you turn to Him in prayer.

The Sit-down

At some point in your relationship, ask your spouse about your mutual vision if you do not have one yet. Now that you know how both of you can arrive at it, take the needed steps I have shared in this chapter, cognizant of the source, elements, and value of a vision for your union. There are no hard and fast rules on how to approach this; you may simply ask the Lord to show it to you, or you both can take some time off to pray, meditate, and fast to bring yourselves in alignment with the Lord and with each other.

Remember, where there is no vision, failure is inevitable. Take time—more so now that you have probably been married for a while and things may not be as you thought they would—to bring your marriage into view as God sees it. It pays for you and your spouse to have a God's eye view of your marriage.

Your Marriage's Mission

Your marriage's mission has to do with the day-to-day of your marriage. It is not enough to write down the vision and make it plain; there must be running. While God's vision for your marriage may be grand, it must cascade into family life, finances, parenting, and, most importantly, how the couple relates with God. It must also align with His purpose for marriage, which, as I have mentioned a few times now, is to reflect His image to the world and raise godly children.

The mission of a marriage is the set of behaviors that arise out of your marriage's vision and purpose; it is what everyone experiences as a direct consequence of your marriage.

From time to time, the Holy Spirit will aid you by supplying new instruction to help you accomplish the vision. The Bible says the Holy Spirit will remind you of the things that God spoke to your hearts as a couple about His desires concerning your union.

The other thing that will make up your mission is your children—biological or spiritual.

"Train up a child in the way he should go, and when he is old he will not depart from it" (Proverbs 22:6).

Make no mistakes about it; God is concerned about your children for the very fact that His vision for you and your spouse is actually transgenerational. Training them in the way that they should go presupposes that you and your spouse know the way. It means teaching your children to grasp your God-given vision and live by it. I find that this practice is one of the factors that make rich families and rich nations.

Hoshi Ryokan is a Japanese hotel business that has been in existence since 718. As at the time of writing, the hotel had marked its 1,300th anniversary, passed from father to son for forty-six generations. Recognized by the *Guinness Book of World Records* as the world's oldest hotel, the secret to their succession accomplishment has been to pass on the leadership of the hotel to the eldest son of each generation so that there is no ambiguity about whom to train. Zengoro Hoshi, the company's current helmsman, will pass the business on to his eldest grandson (the forty-eighth generation), following the demise of his eldest son a few years ago.

All this goes to say that families who prioritize pursuing a vision and succession planning make more impact than families who do not. There is more than enough evidence to support the fact that they practice Proverbs 22:6, seeing that their corporate histories—from the cash-rich Asian family businesses to the globally dominant Mittelstand firms of Germany—are replete with stories of generational transfer of wisdom.

Aside from the mission of training your children, your marriage should serve as a model to other marriages. No marriage is an island. Depending on how the Holy Spirit sees it fit, you and your spouse may be charged with helping other marriages directly or indirectly based on the wisdom and resources with which He has blessed you.

> Jesus said, "*Go therefore and make disciples of all the nations, baptizing them in the name of the Father and of the Son and of the Holy Spirit, teaching them to observe all things that I have commanded you; and lo, I am with you always, even to the end of the age.*" (Matthew 28:19–20)

In other words, go to the married people and make disciples of them in the name of the Father and of the Son and of the Holy Spirit, teaching them to observe that husband and wife are one and not two partners, acknowledging that the Holy Spirit is with you always, even to the very end. Amen.

Chapter 17

The Mandate of Global Dominion

Every marriage is designed for global dominion. Whenever the devil sees a marriage anywhere in the world, no matter the culture or creed, he is reminded of Adam and Eve and their mission. Adam and Eve were Lucifer's replacements as viceroys of Earth after he and his cohorts were banished from heaven (see Revelation 12:4). Though he successfully supplanted them in the Garden of Eden and took back what authority God had granted the couple, his displeasure with humankind stemmed from the fact that God offered amnesty to humankind but not to him.

> *Then God said, "Let Us make man in Our image, according to Our likeness; let them have dominion over the fish of the sea, over the birds of the air, and over the cattle, over all the earth and over every creeping thing that creeps on the earth." So God created man in His own image; in the image of God He created him; male and female He created them. Then God blessed them, and God said to them, "Be fruitful and multiply; fill the earth and subdue it; have dominion over the fish of the sea,*

over the birds of the air, and over every living thing that moves on the earth." (Genesis 1:26–28)

God's original mandate to Adam and Eve to populate the earth still stands today via marriage. Now, more than any time in human history, Satan and his cohorts have waged war on marriage. They know that marriage is the only relationship that can guarantee the raising of a godly people out of the next generation. The severity of the impact of divorce on children—many growing up social delinquents—cannot be overstated.

From imprisonment to drug addiction to mental health trouble, children of divorced parents fare far worse than children whose parents work through the issues and stay together. For instance, according to two separate studies in the US, children of broken marriages are five times more predisposed to mental health issues within a year of their parents' divorce (Nan Marie Astone and Sara S. McLanahan, "Family Structure, Parental Practices and High School Completion," *American Sociological Review* 56 (1991); Cynthia Harper and Sara McLanahan, "Father Absence and Youth Incarceration," Working Paper, Center for Research on Child Wellbeing). They are also more predisposed to suicide later on in life. Moreover, no country on the planet is exempt from this problem.

Marriage will raise individuals who are more balanced, capable of turning to God, no matter the creed or culture in which they are raised. This is true even in societies where the gospel of Jesus Christ is not easily accessible. The prospect of children being raised by both parents in a marriage alone provides Satan with the impetus to fight marriage globally. Coupled with the fact that such children, who are more balanced, could turn to Christ and become effective instruments for evangelizing others, Satan has divorce projected into the global consciousness through mainstream media on a moment-by-moment basis.

Global Design

Just like Adam and Eve, God designed all marriages to have world impact. The very idea that God designed marriage so that humankind could dominate the world is very instructive. What is even more instructive is the agenda of God in Genesis 1:28.

"Then God blessed them, and God said to them, 'Be fruitful and multiply; fill the earth and subdue it; have dominion over the fish of the sea, over the birds of the air, and over every living thing that moves on the earth."

The first couple had never heard any words like these before, yet God said to them, as He says to marriages today, "Be fruitful and multiply."

Now many may think that God was only asking us to be fruitful with our bodies as the birth rates of most of the developing world suggests. However, God was also asking us to be fruitful on four other planes.

As Ghanaian pastor Dr. Mensa Otabil puts it, "God commanded all humanity to bear fruit with our hands, lips, minds, and, lastly, with our spirits."

In other words, aside from producing children, God desires fruit from our hands in the form of work, fruit from our lips in the form of words, fruit from our minds in the form of creativity, and fruit from our spirits in the form of character.

The second part of this mandate is the proliferation part in which God charges us to multiply our fruitfulness until it dominates the entire globe. This is the part that most marriages never discover, let alone display to the earth.

Going by the law of first mention in biblical hermeneutics, God's mandate to the first marriage applies to your marriage today. Adam and Eve, Abraham and Sarah, Boaz and Ruth, Joseph and Mary, and even Aquila and Pricilla all had global impact. You, too, can.

Chapter 18

I Will, Be Healed

Some of the things I am going to write about in this chapter should never even be mentioned among Christians, but they are a reality in some marriages today.

Let us face it—a sizable number of marriages end because of infidelity, domestic abuse, and financial mismanagement. Nothing just happens. People behave as best as they know how, even if their behaviors are self-destructive. As Maya Angelou said, "I did then what I knew how to do. Now that I know better, I do better." This implies that everyone is on a continuum, and the better we know, the better we act. The same holds true for Christians when you consider what the Bible says in 2 Peter 1:2:

"Grace and peace be multiplied to you in the knowledge of God and of Jesus our Lord."

It is by grace and peace that we overcome these kinds of challenges in marriage, but to get grace and peace, you need to first increase your assent to God's Word. What some couples have is not a problem with cheating, domestic violence, or financial mismanagement but a problem with the Word of God—a knowledge problem. These will not go away by fasting and prayers or by reading copious portions of Scripture. It will only respond to what you assent to in the Word of God.

A good illustration of this is the legislative process in many countries by which certain matters of interest become law. In dictatorships, the word of the dictator is law. How he or she feels about anything determines how every other person within his or her domain should feel about it. This is the way many people see God. However, God operates like a legislature. From His willingness to have conversations with Adam and Eve in the cool of the day (see Genesis 3:8) to His frank banter with Sarah when He announced that she would, at old age, conceive and birth Isaac and she laughed in unbelief (see Genesis 18:10–15), we see that God is not the autocrat organized religion portrays Him as. Like legislatures around the world, God originates proposals through His Word and passes them to the executive branch, the church, for assent. Otherwise, why would God say, "*I have set before you life and death, blessing and cursing; therefore choose life, that both you and your descendants may live*"? It is only when we agree with the Word of God that it becomes flesh.

Jesus said, "*Thy will be done in earth, as it is in heaven*" (Matthew 6:10 KJV).

God's will is legislated in heaven and awaits the assent of His church on earth. Paul reiterates this in his letter to Philemon.

He writes:

> *I thank my God, making mention of you always in my prayers, hearing of your love and faith which you have toward the Lord Jesus and toward all the saints, that the sharing of your faith may become effective by the acknowledgment of every good thing which is in you in Christ Jesus.* (Philemon 1:4–6)

This simply means that the quality of life we lead as Christians is a product of our assenting to every good thing that is in us based on our membership of the body of Christ. All effort at becoming better is futile without first assenting to the Word of God. This is the secret of all Christian development.

Assenting to the Jesus message, "So then, they are no longer two but one flesh" (Matthew 19:6) is the place where healing starts for any marriage that has gone through infidelity, domestic violence, and financial abuse. The fact is that all the harm that have come to a husband or wife by the actions of their significant other have come from not agreeing with Jesus on the truth that the two of them are one. Cheating on, beating up, or financially abusing one's spouse is also revelatory of self-ignorance or self-hatred.

Normal people do not just harm themselves. Only the insane, or people without knowledge of the consequences of their self-harming behaviors, afflict themselves. When two people get married, they become a new self. As such, having affairs, being violent with, or financially irresponsible toward a spouse hurts both the perpetrator and the victim in the same visceral way.

The preponderance of these three forms of abuse, among other factors, makes it easy to conclude that divorces do not just happen. First, the marriages get sick from poisonous thinking and then slowly die off. The infidelity, domestic violence, and financial abuse that are rife today are only symptoms of sick marriages.

> *Now a leper came to Him, imploring Him, kneeling down to Him and saying to Him, "If You are willing, You can make me clean." Then Jesus, moved with compassion, stretched out His hand and touched him, and said to him, "I am willing; be cleansed." As soon as He had spoken, immediately the leprosy left him, and he was cleansed.* (Mark 1:40–42)

Like this leper, God is willing to touch sick marriages but it must start with the willingness of couples to define marriage based on how God defines it.

> *And He answered and said to them, "Have you not read that He who made them at the beginning 'made them male and female,' and said, 'For this reason a man shall leave his father and mother and be joined to his wife, and the two shall become*

one flesh'? So then, they are no longer two but one flesh. Therefore what God has joined together, let not man separate." (Matthew 19:4–6)

God sees His fully-formed image in the husband-and-wife relationship. This is why doing anything that frustrates the union frustrates God (this is clear when you compare Genesis 1:26–28 and Malachi 2:10–16 with Matthew 19:4–6). Infidelity, domestic violence, and financial mismanagement provide sufficient threat to any marriage in the sense that both husband and wife ultimately feel the hurt. If a man or woman cheats, beats up, or financially abuses a spouse, it is because he or she entertains thoughts of not being what God has said he or she is, which has been Satan's oldest trick for decimating humankind.

Satan's Modus Operandi

Satan's modus operandi has always been to offer contrarian thoughts to the Word of God on every subject. His position about marriage is no exception.

When God made Adam and Eve, He made them in His image and likeness. Then He put Adam (with Eve still inside him) in the Garden of Eden and charged them not to eat the fruit of a certain tree of the knowledge of good and evil in the garden, stating death as the consequence of flouting His instruction.

Eve's encounter, chronicled in Genesis 3:1–7, shows that Adam and Eve had conversed about God's instruction after God had taken her out of him. Yet Satan's first order of business was to ask, "Has God indeed said, 'You shall not eat of every tree of the garden'?" To this, Eve responds, *"We may eat the fruit of the trees of the garden; but of the fruit of the tree which is in the midst of the garden, God has said, 'You shall not eat it, nor shall you touch it, lest you die."* This suggests that Satan will query the truth of God's Word in your marriage. He will always project thoughts that suggest you and your spouse are partners, separate entities, to plague your marriage.

Satan then retorts, "*You will not surely die. For God knows that in the day you eat of it your eyes will be opened and you will be like God, knowing good and evil.*" Eve lusts after the fruit based on Satan's word. She is tempted at all three points: the lust of the flesh, the lust of the eyes, and the pride of life. She reaches for it and takes a bite out of it. All this while Adam is not in another part of the garden, tending to business. He is with Eve, observing events when he should have been standing up to Satan.

When Eve gives Adam the fruit and he eats, Satan's coup is complete. "*Then the eyes of both of them were opened, and they knew that they were naked; and they sewed fig leaves together and made themselves coverings*" (Genesis 3:7). Satan knew that Adam and Eve were one. He knew that to dominate them, he had to treat them as two separate entities. He initiated conversation with Eve while relegating Adam to the background, which is what extramarital affairs do to couples today.

Satan also understood that he had to separate them from identifying with God, even though the creator made them in His image and likeness. He attacked their self-worth by leading them away from their dominion into thinking they needed to become like God. This is the same thing he uses domestic violence and financial abuse to accomplish today. Eve may have been deceived because she was still inside Adam when God told them not to eat of that tree, but Adam knew exactly what would happen.

Apostle Paul corroborates, "*For Adam was formed first, then Eve. And Adam was not deceived, but the woman being deceived, fell into transgression*" (1 Timothy 2:13–14).

Adam willfully flouted God's instruction while relinquishing the dominion given to human beings by God. The victor had been victimized, and it is still the same today. Man's disobedience remains the mother of spiritual death and divorce, separation from God and spouse.

For Satan (then Lucifer), he had finally gotten back, by stealth, part of what he lost by his rebellion against God. The saga in the Garden of Eden, where he made Adam and Eve sin against God, was very personal to him. According to Ezekiel 28:11–19, Satan had been the first administrator of the Garden of Eden, from where he possibly ran the rest of earth.

> *You were the seal of perfection, full of wisdom and perfect in beauty. You were in Eden, the garden of God; every precious stone was your covering: the sardius, topaz, and diamond, beryl, onyx, and jasper, sapphire, turquoise, and emerald with gold. The workmanship of your timbrels and pipes was prepared for you on the day you were created. You were the anointed cherub who covers; I established you; you were on the holy mountain of God; you walked back and forth in the midst of fiery stones. You were perfect in your ways from the day you were created, till iniquity was found in you.* (Ezekiel 28:12–15)

God found corruption in Lucifer and deposed him, necessitating a replacement, which would be human beings created in the image and likeness of God—Adam and Eve. Therefore, by causing Adam and Eve to disobey God in Eden, Lucifer not only usurped all the dominion that God had given them to administer earth but he also mocked God for picking humankind over him.

Satan took back the controls of the earth and even flaunted it at Jesus in the last of the three documented temptations of Christ.

> *Then the devil, taking Him up on a high mountain, showed Him all the kingdoms of the world in a moment of time. And the devil said to Him, "All this authority I will give You, and their glory; for this has been delivered to me, and I give it to whomever I wish."* (Luke 4:5–6)

It was not enough that Satan became the god of this world (see 2 Corinthians 4:4); mocking God became his chief pastime from that day in the Garden of Eden until now. For this reason, Satan hates marriage because it reminds him of the image of God.

God says, "Let us," but Satan says, "I will," which in a sense are clear indicators of the spirits behind marriage and divorce. God collaborates with human beings and encourages them to collaborate with each other, but Satan manipulatively tyrannizes humankind and instigates people to dominate others.

X-raying how infidelity, domestic violence, and financial misappropriation are not just bad behavioral choices but active weapons of Satan for dismembering marriages and ruining generations should form part of the corpus of knowledge that intending couples have long before getting married. One cannot gainsay the importance of having conversations about sex, abuse, and money with an intended, even at the preliminary stages of the relationship, no matter how difficult these conversations are. More than this, both parties, seeking to become parts of each other, need to agree on a remedy should any of the three occur during the course of their marriage.

Note that no one ever gets married to get divorced. If you are already married and you have not had this talk with your spouse, do not assume that both of you are on the same page and way beyond any crisis.

"*Therefore let him who thinks he stands take heed lest he fall*" (2 Corinthians 10:12).

Infidelity

Extramarital affairs are most often the cause of divorce. But why do people cheat? They cheat because they desire to—most times, not knowing what the implications are.

> *Let no one say when he is tempted, "I am tempted by God"; for God cannot be tempted by evil, nor does He Himself tempt anyone. But each one is tempted when he is drawn away by his own desires and enticed. Then, when desire has conceived, it*

gives birth to sin; and sin, when it is full-grown, brings forth death. (James 1:13–15)

Sometimes, it is about self-loathing masked with adventure, and at other times, revenge is the motivation. Whichever it is, infidelity manifests because of two reasons:

- A lack of self-knowledge, and
- A self-hatred that accompanies not accepting your new self after you get married.

Lack of Self-knowledge

If a person gets married, he or she becomes a new self with his or her spouse. The two are no longer two but one. The onus on married couples is understanding the ramifications of their oneness from how each part deals with a varied number of issues—down to details as minute as when one spouse prefers to make love. Being open and learning about your new self is the most important duty in marriage.

However, many view their spouses as partners separate from themselves—and this is the first fault point for infidelity. Now, I am writing to Christians, and I understand that no believer will go out of his way to cheat on a spouse without the conviction of his or her conscience before and after the deed.

However, it pays to understand the operations of the enemy. Just as Satan isolated Eve from Adam, the lure to cheat, whether it starts with a look, conversation, or online interaction, always singles out its victim to create rapport while relegating the spouse. As psychologist Esther Perel rightly observed, "The constitutive element of infidelity is the secrecy." This is why you must embrace the idea of oneness with your spouse so that nothing is even able to come in between you and your spouse.

The second chink in the armor, when it comes to infidelity, is your eyesight. Satan seeks to control your eyes because they are the fastest route into your soul. The appeal of Hollywood is one of Satan's tools to gain control of your eyes.

"So when the woman saw that the tree was good for food; that it was pleasant to the eyes, and a tree desirable to make one wise, she took of its fruit and ate. She also gave to her husband with her, and he ate" (Genesis 3:6).

What Eve saw led to a sequence of events that made her and her husband literally become unfaithful to God. "The eyes are the light of the body," Jesus said in Matthew 6:22 to mean, the eyes are a source of consciousness. What we become conscious of, we possess the ability to bring about. Quantum physicists agree that until observed, everything exists as potential. This is why Jesus said, *"That whoever looks at a woman to lust for her has already committed adultery with her in his heart"* (Matthew 5:28). It does not matter that it is a man or woman, the chemistry involved in looking desirously into the eyes of another, who is not your spouse, can count as infidelity in some cases and is the precursor to the next fault point for infidelity: rapport.

Once a person establishes rapport with another, whom he or she is unable to tell a spouse about, an affair is in progress. Whether the rapport develops from long-secluded conversations, chats on the phone, or secret rendezvous with online dating apps, affairs—albeit emotional at first, usually morph into sexual relationships with the attendant complications. The truth is, married people, who do this often, create uncanny monstrosities by bringing their spouses—unbeknownst to them—into another marriage, thereby dishonoring the image of God.

It is no wonder that infidelity is the leading cause of divorce, and this does not take into account the other problems associated with polygamous behavior. Unfaithful people do not just cheat on their spouses; they cheat on their new self in the most inordinate way. Esther Perel calls it "the shattering of the self," such that the cheated spouse can no longer trust the cheat or their own selves. All preconceptions about their relationship wash away at the discovery of infidelity, and as with a head misaligned from its body or vice versa, pain becomes the order of the day. Pain may take the form of guilt, rage, depression, or a combination of two or all three for either or both spouses—the cheat and the cheated on—but it seldom leaves them unscathed. In fact, studies show that divorce is more likely to occur from the aftereffects of an affair than the affair itself.

The truth is there is just too much at stake in marriage, making the lure to cheat a crappy offering. Satan goes beyond ruining a person's reputation with infidelity. He attacks everything—from your reason for being to the well-being of everyone connected to you and your spouse, even several generations after.

David's tryst with Bathsheba bore direct correlation to his firstborn, Amnon's incest with his half sister, Tamar (2 Samuel 13:1–14), the rebellions of Absalom (2 Samuel 16:22) and Adonijah (1 Kings 1:5–31), and the eventual secession of northern Israel during the reign of his grandson, Rehoboam.

Like a malware, infidelity is a tool used by Satan to cause systemic havoc in society, which is why it pays to know yourself and the kind of enemy we face. Imagine a head with more than one body or a body with more than one head. This is almost exactly what happens when a man cheats on his wife or a woman cheats on her husband.

Sun Tzu said:

> If you know the enemy and know yourself, you need not fear the result of a hundred battles. If you know yourself but not the enemy, for every victory gained you will also suffer a defeat. If you know neither the enemy nor yourself, you will succumb in every battle.

It is no wonder King Solomon writes, "*Whoever commits adultery with a woman lacks understanding; he who does so destroys his own soul*" (Proverbs 6:32).

Domestic Violence

Statistics have shown that domestic violence is a leading cause of death for women globally. About 55 percent of the killings of women in the United States between 2003 and 2014 were domestic violence–related, according to the Centers for Disease Control and Prevention.

The Office for National Statistics in the United Kingdom reports that about 1.9 million people (1.2 million women and 713,000 men) experienced domestic violence between March 2016 and March 2017 in England and Wales. The report also accounts that two women are murdered by a partner or ex-partner every week.

In other parts of the world, the statistics are even grimmer with the number of women, who suffer domestic violence, ranging between 60 to 80 percent in parts of Africa and Asia, according to a study conducted by the United Nations.

Violence is often an offshoot of insecurity, which, in itself, is the product of lack of self-knowledge. Violent husbands and wives simply do not assent to being one with their spouses; otherwise, they would not hit them.

> *"For this reason a man shall leave his father and mother and be joined to his wife, and the two shall become one flesh"? So then, they are no longer two but one flesh. Therefore what God has joined together, let not man separate.* (Matthew 19:5–6)

"For no one ever hated his own flesh" (Ephesians 5:29).

Rightly dividing Matthew 19:5 with Ephesians 5:29 sums it all for us. Husbands or wives who batter their spouses do not see themselves as one with their victims for the very fact that no one victimizes himself or herself. Violent people fight with monsters from their abusive pasts, whether it is someone, a group of people, an event, or series of events. They grapple with a gnawing lie that they are not enough and, sadly, because of ignorance, carry on with it into marriage.

"He who fights with monsters might take care lest he thereby become a monster. And if you gaze for long into an abyss, the abyss gazes also into you" (Friedrich Nietzsche).

The illusion of abuse is the monster that Satan uses to trigger abuse among Christians, which is why I will advise professional counseling and Scripture meditation. Counseling will help pinpoint the source of illusion, while meditation will help you see the complete image God has of you.

Financial Misappropriation

Money tells you everything you need to know about a person. In fact, it is an indicator of whether a couple are codependent, collaborating as partners or vitally one entity.

Remember, we said Satan's primary strategy is to separate and isolate one spouse from the other. When a spouse is not forthcoming about money, maybe hides an expenditure or debt, it could be termed financial infidelity. We cannot belabor the fact that keeping any secrets from one's spouse is all the gunpowder that the enemy needs to blow a marriage to smithereens. Being unable to account for financial resources is the number one sign that a marriage is in trouble. I understand that many may feel uncomfortable here, but if your spouse does not know every cent that you earn and vice versa, you are not in the state of marriage that God had in mind for you from the foundation of the world. In fact, you are either financially abusing your spouse or permitting financial abuse.

Now, I am for full disclosure before marriage, but if that does not happen then, it must take place after the couple have said, "I do," because they are one entity now.

In Japanese culture, the practice of husbands giving their wives their monthly income to manage is prevalent. This culture of money management being the wife's prerogative has been passed down for thousands of years, not so she can henpeck her husband but to promote transparency between them. It is worthy of note that the divorce rate in Japan has remained significantly low when compared to the rest of the world.

As Gwen Guthrie said, "No romance without finance." The facts stand: men without money are less susceptible to cheating and so are women who feel financially secure. Husbands, I am not saying hand your money to your wives, no. However, live with your spouse in such a way that neither of you is ever in doubt as to where your financial resources flow. One could be well-intentioned and still not be transparent. That charitable gift, which your spouse is not aware of, is tantamount to cheating.

The point is, without financial accountability, there is no marriage. Being unaccountable to your spouse is how every evil that occurs in a marriage finds root. An undisclosed bonus at work could be the window that Satan uses to tempt you to lust, leading you to consummate a secret sin.

Being one entity means that there are no spats about *his* money or *her* money. In fact, thinking of money in such terms only means that the enemy has successfully separated you using money. There is no telling how many marriages are like this.

Remedies

Infidelity, domestic violence, and financial mismanagement are actually symptoms of the same root cause: the nonacceptance of what marriage is according to the Jesus message. We can make a long list of remedies you can use to resolve these situations, if any or all of them have reared their ugly heads in your marriage, but only one thing is needful: submission.

You both have to agree to submit the three things you have—your consciousness, time, and environment—to Jesus Christ.

Submitting Your Consciousness

Submitting your consciousness to the Lord means that you become conversant with living as though you and your spouse are extensions of each other. It is the ingrained cognizance of the *we*-ness of marriage such that everything that you (husband and wife) do carries the endorsement of Jesus's words, "No longer two but one."

Submitting your consciousness means meditating on or becoming aware of Matthew 19:5–6 such that you and your spouse become the manifestation of the words, known and read by everyone.

Submitting Your Time

Submitting your time to Jesus means fellowship. It means you agree to sit together periodically with the Lord to transparently talk and pray about the different issues as they pertain to your marriage. You could also use these times to draw up financial budgets or conduct financial reviews. Having sessions in which you acknowledge your oneness with your spouse, in agreement with the Lord, actually honors Him in such a way that it reinforces that oneness and the potency of your marriage's vision.

Malachi 2:15 states, *"But did He not make them one, having a remnant of the Spirit? And why one? He seeks godly offspring. Therefore take heed to your spirit, and let none deal treacherously with the wife of his youth."*

Time spent nurturing your oneness in open conversation and prayer will end deliberate hurt in your marriage.

Submitting Your Environment

There are people you should not be with, and there are places you should not be at. Submitting your environment to Jesus means changing your associations and the places you visit that predispose your marriage to collapse. There is a reason God asked us not to keep company with fornicating Christians (1 Corinthians 5:9) or ungodly people (1 Corinthians 15:33).

"A little leaven leavens the whole lump" (Galatians 5:9).

Knowing that Satan wants to cut you off from your spouse to mock God is not enough. You have to be deliberate about preventing it from happening by submitting your environment to the Lord. Choose your company wisely, listen to the leading of the Holy Spirit, and always watch out for people who do not endorse the Jesus-position on marriage. People who do not see themselves as one with their spouses leave a back door for Satan to come in and take them away from their spouses eventually. It is irrelevant that they are your parents, friends, or mentors; what they believe is contagious. Be careful.

The Healing Balm

God wants to heal many marriages undergoing all kinds of turmoil right now. However, two cannot walk together, except when they agree. God needs you to agree with His Son on your marriage right now. You may have read up until this point and not yet wholly agreed with the Lord that a husband is one with his wife, yet this is the only way Jesus can heal a marriage.

It does not matter what you have believed about marriage for so many years if it does not concur with Jesus's position.

> *And He answered and said to them, "Have you not read that He who made them at the beginning 'made them male and female,' and said, 'For this reason a man shall leave his father and mother and be joined to his wife, and the two shall become one flesh'? So then, they are no longer two but one flesh. Therefore what God has joined together, let not man separate."* (Matthew 19:4–6)

This is all you need to piece your marriage together. Shifting your mind about who your spouse is to you will alter your prayer life, the way you communicate with each other, and how both of you approach other aspects of your life.

Affirm it with your mouth, believing in your heart that you and your spouse are one. Ask the Lord to help you realize this oneness with your spouse at the core of your being and never again entertain any thoughts, words, or actions that put him or her outside your identity.

Chapter 19

An Appeal for Intercession We Wrestle Not—

Because Satan is utterly distraught over what marriage represents in the spirit realm, he would stop at nothing to break as many marriages as he can. Using suggestions and philosophies that contradict the Word of God, Satan has tanked many marriages over the years to stop certain generations from fulfilling destiny. He is enthralled—spiritually speaking—by the images of headless bodies and bodiless heads lying lifeless. When Christians deteriorate in marriage relationships and head to the divorce courts, he can mock God with great relish and say, "There goes your image, God."

Yet Christians are often ignorant of the enjoyment that Satan derives when a marriage dies.

We have said that God designed marriage to populate the earth with godly people. However, Satan inflicts enormous damage on the community with divorce. Nobody actually escapes. From the couple, their children and their extended family members, to their Christian brethren, friends, and neighbors—all partake in the consequences, one way or another.

This is why interceding for marriages is a primary duty for Christians, particularly couples. If Satan is so serious about tanking marriages because of his desire to mock God and weaken the mission of the church, saving marriages ought to be a Christian priority.

Take time to pray for this message—that it will save many marriages, that oneness will become the predominant thought in marriages now troubled by stressors, and that many will use their realization of oneness with Jesus to forge oneness in their marriages.

Take a moment from this book and talk to the Lord right now.

Pray that Christians across the world will be awakened to God's desire to realize godly seeds through marriage—that they will muster the inner strength to endure the cross of marriage and pursue the glory of God through their unions. Pray for marriages riddled with infidelity, violence, and extravagance—that a realization of the meaning of marriage will intensify, so much so that such behaviors will become a thing of the past.

It does not matter if it was your marriage you prayed about or the marriage of someone you know. I have a witness in my heart that a turnaround has begun, and you will surely testify of it in Jesus's name. Amen.

Chapter 20

Christ and His Church

In his book *Maps of Meaning*, Jordan B. Peterson juxtaposes femininity with masculinity using both amorphous and easily recognizable schema. Using the Taoist philosophical symbolization of yin and yang to depict the interconnectedness of everything, his work gives insight into the oneness of certain-paired phenomena, categorizing them into masculine and feminine. Humanity and Mother Nature, husband and wife, and Christ and the church are all cascades of yin and yang in the sense that, despite the differences of traits of the paired components, they are only able to achieve their God-ordained purpose together.

In ontology (the branch of philosophy that studies being), this concept of the plurality of things is termed *dualistic monism*. Peterson highlights the positive aspects of each of the parts and the negative aspects, particularly when a member of the pair runs solo without the modifying effect of its other part. For example, nature is feminine. Nature is capable of nurture, creativity, and fecundity on the positive side. Whereas on the negative side, nature is capable of wanton destruction, especially in the absence of its compatible masculine—humanity. This is the same case for wives without husbands and the church without Christ, such that single mothers are more likely to nurture children who end up becoming menaces to society, while churches lacking submission to Christ, who is the Word of God, morph into dangerous cults.

Masculinity, on the other hand, is the source of order on the positive side. God tasked Adam and Eve with governing earth, naming the animals and procreating. If you have noticed, all book long, I have refrained from using the term *mankind* to describe human beings because of the idea that its usage is sexist, but this is exactly what humans are to Mother Nature. Human beings are her masculine part.

"*Then God blessed them, and God said to them, "be fruitful and multiply; fill the earth and subdue it; have dominion over the fish of the sea, over the birds of the air, and over every living thing that moves on the earth*" (Genesis 1:28).

The negative aspect of masculinity, if allowed free rein without the interplay of its feminine counterpart, is tyranny. The consequence of tyrannical masculinity is critical or destructive femininity. Femininity pushes back to tone down unbridled masculinity. This is the cause of the rise of feminism in countries where male domination once held sway—from the Me Too movement in North America to the clamor for women drivers in Saudi Arabia. The COP21 Paris agreement signed by 195 countries under the auspices of the United Nations Framework Convention on Climate Change is actually humanity (masculine), attempting to lower its tyranny of Mother Nature (feminine) to avert her wanton destruction.

Yin and yang offer an indisputable understanding of how the husband and wife relate to Christ and the church such that it is easy to diagnose the health of our marriages and the health of our Christianity by merely observing the interplay of the components of each.

When a husband and wife fail to recognize their oneness, domination and subservience become the dynamic of their marriage, regardless of whether their marriage is in a state of codependency or partnership. This is the root of every evil in marriage.

Likewise, when Christians fail to recognize their oneness with the Lord or when they accept false christs, domination and subservience become the dynamic of their Christian experience. For the most part, this has been the experience of the majority of Christian folk across the world since 325 AD when the institutional church began.

What does it mean for Christians to recognize their oneness with Christ? It means that each of us sees ourselves as part of Christ and not apart from Him. It means that we share everything with the Almighty God as much as He shares everything with us.

This is why Jesus came. He came to live with us through our everyday experience while we sit with Him in His heavenly experience. This is a fact that does not only read well on the pages of Scripture but vitally in our hearts.

> *But God, who is rich in mercy, because of His great love with which He loved us, even when we were dead in trespasses, made us alive together with Christ* [by grace you have been saved], *and raised us up together, and made us sit together in the heavenly places in Christ Jesus, that in the ages to come He might show the exceeding riches of His grace in His kindness toward us in Christ Jesus. For by grace you have been saved through faith, and that not of yourselves; it is the gift of God, not of works, lest anyone should boast. For we are His workmanship, created in Christ Jesus for good works, which God prepared beforehand that we should walk in them.* (Ephesians 2:4–10)

When God said, "Behold, the virgin shall conceive and bear a Son, and shall call His name Immanuel" (in Isaiah 7:14), He was expressing a desire to be with us forever.

> *And Jesus came and spoke to them, saying, "All authority has been given to Me in heaven and on earth. Go therefore and make disciples of all the nations, baptizing them in the name of the Father and of the Son and of the Holy Spirit, teaching them to observe all things that I have commanded you;*

and lo, I am with you always, even to the end of the age." Amen. (Matthew 28:18–20)

This means, the Christian dwells with Jesus inside his or her body. It also means that everywhere they go, Jesus goes. If you are a Christian, you and the Lord reside together in your body. He has the first say because He is flawless, while you concur. Your oneness with Jesus may not always be apparent, but it starts when you confess His lordship and get baptized in water. From that point, you became a new entity that did not exist before (see 2 Corinthians 5:17). What belongs to Jesus now belongs to you and vice versa. In a sense, you are now married to the Lord—hence the many references to the church as the bride of Christ (John 3:29, 2 Corinthians 11:2, Revelation 19:7–9, Revelation 21:2, 9–11).

Just to be clear, the church is not the building Christians go to on Sundays. The church is who we are—the called out ones, the people with whom God makes His home.

"The Spirit Himself bears witness with our spirit that we are children of God, and if children, then heirs—heirs of God and joint heirs with Christ, if indeed we suffer with Him, that we may also be glorified together" (Romans 8:16–17).

We are joint heirs with Christ. This means that we share with Him a mutuality of everything. If Jesus is the heir of all things (according to Hebrews 1:1–2), then we, too, are heirs with Him. More strikingly, He shares our spirits, souls, and bodies such that we should not make decisions without Him as He does not make decisions without us.

As evangelist T. L. Osborn once said, "God needs me as much as I need Him." This is a visceral truth about Christ and His church; we can only advance God's will on earth by being in constant communion with Him. Christ is the head, and we are His body.

"How do Christians accept false christs?" one might ask. The answer to this question will explain to a great degree the tyrannies that have been perpetrated in the name of the Lord Jesus Christ for centuries—from the time of the dark ages to today's prosperity gospel smoke screen that many have become accustomed to.

If you have not put this book down by now, I want to encourage you to continue and allow me to provide answers to certain dysfunctionalities that have been associated with our faith.

"The Grand Inquisitor" is a prose poem in Fyodor Dostoevsky's novel *the Brothers Karamazov* that provides ample provender to satisfy the curious mind. Told by Ivan Karamazov to his brother Alyosha, a novice monk, the tale shows an interplay between Christ, false christs (in the form of organized religion), and the church.

In this parable, Christ returns to earth in Seville at the time of the Spanish Inquisition. He performs a number of miracles, reminiscent of miracles from the gospels. The people recognize Jesus and worship Him at the Seville Cathedral, but He is arrested by Inquisition leaders and sentenced to burn at the stake the next day. The Grand Inquisitor visits the Lord in His cell to tell Him that the church no longer needs Him. The Inquisitor goes on to explain to Jesus why His return would interfere with the mission of the church.

The Inquisitor anchors his denunciation of Jesus on the three questions that Satan asked Jesus during His temptation in the wilderness—the temptation to turn stones into bread, the temptation to cast Himself from the Temple's pinnacle and be rescued by the angels, and the temptation to rule over all the kingdoms of this world. The Inquisitor states that Jesus declined these three temptations in favor of freedom, but the Inquisitor thinks that Jesus is wrong about human nature. He does not believe that the vast majority of humanity can handle the freedom which Jesus has given them. The Inquisitor then implies that Jesus, by giving humans the freedom to choose, has excluded the majority of humanity from redemption and doomed it to suffer.

Despite declaring the Inquisitor to be an unbeliever, Ivan also quotes the Inquisitor as saying that the Catholic Church follows "the wise spirit, the dread spirit of death and destruction." The old Inquisitor says, "We are not with Thee, but with him, and that is our secret! For centuries have we abandoned Thee to follow him." For he, through compulsion, provided the tools to end all human suffering and for humanity to unite under the banner of the church. The multitude then is guided through the church by the few who are strong enough to handle the burden of freedom. The Inquisitor boasts that, under him, all mankind will live and die happily in ignorance. Though he leads them only to "death and destruction," they will be happy along the way. The Inquisitor will be a self-martyr, spending his life to keep choice from humanity. He states that "anyone who can appease a man's conscience can take his freedom away from him."

The Inquisitor furthers this argument by explaining why Christ was wrong to decline each temptation by Satan. According to him, Christ should have turned stones into bread because men will always follow those who will feed their bellies. The Inquisitor recalls how Christ rejected this, saying, "Man cannot live on bread alone," and explains to Christ:

> Feed men and then ask of them virtue! That's what they'll write on the banner they'll raise against Thee and with which they will destroy Thy temple. Where Thy temple stood will rise a new building; the terrible tower of Babel will be built again, and though, like the one of old, it will not be finished.

Casting Himself down from the temple to be caught by angels would solidify His godhood in the minds of people, who would follow Him forever. Ruling over all the kingdoms of the earth would assure the people of their salvation, the Grand Inquisitor claims.

The segment ends when Christ, who has been silent throughout, kisses the Inquisitor on his "bloodless, aged lips," instead of answering him. On this, the Inquisitor releases Christ but tells Him never to return. Christ, still silent, leaves through the dark alleys of the city. Not only is the kiss strange, but its effect on the Inquisitor is as well. Ivan concludes: "The kiss burns in his heart, but the old man adheres to his idea."

Christ is the righteous masculine. He is the only source of order in the church. His is an integrative approach.

> *How is it then, brethren? Whenever you come together, each of you has a psalm, has a teaching, has a tongue, has a revelation, has an interpretation. Let all things be done for edification. If anyone speaks in a tongue, let there be two or at the most three, each in turn, and let one interpret. But if there is no interpreter, let him keep silent in church, and let him speak to himself and to God. Let two or three prophets speak, and let the others judge. But if anything is revealed to another who sits by, let the first keep silent. For you can all prophesy one by one, that all may learn and all may be encouraged. And the spirits of the prophets are subject to the prophets. For God is not the author of confusion but of peace, as in all the churches of the saints.* (1 Corinthians 14:26–33)

Organized religion, represented by the old Inquisitor, is the negative masculine. Claiming to produce order, it is the source of tyranny. It is the false Christ, instituting a clergy and a laity to decapitate the church, when Christ bequeathed the priesthood to Christians. Organized religion does not believe the church can handle 1 Corinthians 14:26–33, so it supplants Christ with itself to control Christ's body.

Using the lust of the flesh, the lust of the eye, and the pride of life to tempt the body as he did the head, Satan is unveiled as the architect of organized religion. Rather than every joint (Christians) supplying love from the head to foster real growth, according to Ephesians 4:16, organized religion would rather be a strongman (whether it is a bishop, priest, or pastor), a choir—and other officials, in roles that have no bearing from scripture, feed the lusts of the people.

In a sense, the church has committed acts of infidelity against Christ with organized religion. This has been Satan's greatest onslaught against God in our day, always seeking to decimate His image on earth. The power structures, the chasing after position, and other artificial paraphernalia prevalent in the institutional church ultimately betray human lust and the real architect of organized religion.

Christ and His church, on the other hand, are people. On a granular level, every Christian is the church, the body headed by Jesus Christ Himself, not a pope or a pastor. We are all priests, able to share in the priesthood of our high priest without intermediaries. The same glory Jesus shared with God, He shares with us (see John 17:22).

> *And Jesus came and spoke to them, saying, "All authority has been given to Me in heaven and on earth. Go therefore and make disciples of all the nations, baptizing them in the name of the Father and of the Son and of the Holy Spirit, teaching them to observe all things that I have commanded you; and lo, I am with you always, even to the end of the age."* (Matthew 28:18–20)

While organized religion causes the church to lust and eventually destroys the lives of some, Christ causes the church to give. Organized religion, like every other institution, was set up for the benefit of the few, whereas every member of Christ's church is relevant, has a psalm, a teaching, a tongue, a skill, or something for the benefit of the whole.

While organized religion uses domination to achieve its agenda, Christ, like His Father, is integrative. He is in all and fills all (see Ephesians 1:23). Organized religion says money will send the gospel around the world, but Jesus says it is love that will do it.

Organized religion causes the church to focus on fallen human nature, but Jesus Christ would have His church focus on the union.

We are not the first Adam but the second and last Adam. We are not living souls but life-giving spirits. As Christ is, so are we in this world.

Organized religion makes us seem separate from God and needing clergy to go between, but this is a lie. Christ is with us forever such that we have all things in common with Him. There is no middle wall of separation between Him and us. We are one. I pray that many would grasp this and walk out of bondages they have allowed to hold them down for years. If Christ could not be sick, then we (Jesus and I) cannot be sick. If Christ is the heir of all things, then we (Jesus and I) cannot be broke, and so on.

Organized religion, like a wicked husband, has tyrannized the church for centuries because the church refused to submit to its real husband. Jesus has said, "I will never leave nor forsake you" so that we may say with confidence, "The Lord is my helper; I will not be afraid. What can men do to me?" He will never divorce His church. Rather, we must yield ourselves to His lordship in all decisions. Only then will we understand the relationship between Christ and His church and husband and wife.

In the end, Christianity boils down to one word—*we*. This is what marriage expresses, and everything else departs from truth.

Chapter 21

A Personal Word

When I was much younger in my marriage, I used to think that marriage was a partnership. That was all I heard in my formative years, but it was wrong. Marriage is a union: the coming together of two spirits, two souls, and two bodies—man and wife—into a kind of oneness.

A rudimentary way to illustrate this would be to empty a can of Coke and a can of Fanta into the same container. I used to love this mixture as a little boy. Moreover, part of growing up in Nigeria with my younger brother entailed concocting the Coke and Fanta mixture each time we got permission from our parents to take a soda from the fridge. I remember taking a Coke and he a Fanta, or vice versa, and then deciding that, just because we wanted to taste our sodas mixed, I'd pour a little of mine in his cup while he would pour a little of his in mine. It was the unique taste to our palates—this composite taste of Coke and Fanta—that epitomized our connectedness, not either of the sodas on its own. Marriage is, in some way, like that.

One thing you would most certainly leave off reading this book with is the idea that marriage is not a partnership. Partnerships are dissoluble. They connote the idea of an arrangement of two or more people coming together for a purpose; failing which, the partnership disbands. This fundamental thinking about marriage has been the reason for the high divorce rates all over the world.

The second thing is that marriage is not a codependency. A codependent marriage is like a hospital where one spouse—most often the wife—has to play nurse perpetually, such that their marriage is a living hell. I see this a lot with men, who have not fully submitted to God in their roles as husband, priest, and bread provider. Sometimes, these men foolishly compete with their wives, whom God gave them to help fulfill destiny, and at other times, they relinquish the leadership of their families to the very woman to whom they were supposed to mirror the love and headship of God. It is unnatural. Everything rises and falls on leadership; a husband determines whether a marriage succeeds or fails. The eyes are in the head, and it is where the head goes that the body follows.

Call it archaic if you like, but the idea that marriage should be a "till death do us part" phenomenon is a vital one that not only projects divine order but the very image of God. To conclude, allow me to leave you with a few salient thoughts that have been covered in the course of this book.

Marriage Is "Us," Not "You and I"

Marriage is an "us" relationship, not a "you and I" one. While I would not concern myself with whether you are Trinitarian or Unitarian, we can agree that, at the creation of humanity, God said, "Let us make man in our own image and after our likeness." He manifested the plurality of His oneness and the oneness of His plurality when the scriptures said, "And God created man in His image, male and female created He them."

Marriage Is About Agreement

Looking at the relationship Christians have with Jesus Christ and using it to draw parallels with the relationship between husband and wife unravels a simple secret: marriage is about agreement. Nothing about the Christian life is forced, but the Christian must give his or her consent to have a fulfilling relationship with Jesus Christ. Romans 10:9–10 says:

> *If you confess with your mouth the Lord Jesus and believe in your heart that God has raised Him from the dead, you will be saved. For with the heart one believes unto righteousness, and with the mouth confession is made unto salvation.*

The words translated *confess* and *confession* are from the Greek word *homologia*, which means "to consent." In other words, to enjoy salvation—God's provision for His children in Jesus Christ—we must give God our consent.

Children Are the Expression of the Union

Children are not the objective of a marriage, but bringing them up in godly fashion is. Moreover, it takes a compacted union of father and mother to raise godly children.

Approaching marriage as though children were more important than the union is counter-Scripture. Some parents dote on their children at the expense of properly catering to the health of their marriages because of ignorance. Failing to acknowledge that they and their spouses are one, they self-immolate and, eventually, ruin their families for many generations.

It is no wonder some marriages collapse, following the death of a child. Women are usually the guiltier party when it comes to prizing children over their spouses, even though some men are also guilty of this.

The flood of oxytocin that mothers get at childbirth establishes a lifelong chemical attachment between them and their children. However, love is not attachment, and attachment is not love. Now I do not mean that mothers do not love their children. I refer here to the basis from which some mothers derive their decisions when it comes to their children versus their husbands.

Love is hard. It is sacrificial, and it will test your sanity sometimes. Love is usually based on how much the man is pouring into the marriage from what he has received from the Lord. Attachment, on the other hand, facilitates self-worth, such that mothers, aside from the love they have for their child, also draw self-importance from being needed as a mother. This self-importance reinforces the love of a mother for her children as distinguished from the love for her husband, which, for the lack of a better word, is more spiritually induced.

Infidelity, Domestic Violence and Lack of Financial Accountability Are the Fruits of Self-hatred

Married Christians, who practice any of these three, do not know who they are. In any case, people who do not know who they are cannot love themselves, let alone others. Men and women, who cheat on their spouse, beat them up, or misappropriate funds do not know who they are. Largely, ignorance modifies their behaviors. The same ignorance is why their marriages end up in the sinkholes of divorce courts.

Don't Fire Your Spouse—Have an Intervention

I do not know if you have ever heard this before, but divorce counts for nothing in a marriage, except your spouse is not a believer. If he or she is a Christian and you divorce, you both are still married despite the existence of a divorce certificate.

This is why Jesus said, *"Whoever divorces his wife and marries another commits adultery; and whoever marries her who is divorced from her husband commits adultery"* (Luke 16:18).

Paul corroborates this as a direct instruction from the Lord in 1 Corinthians 7:10–13 where he writes:

> *Now to the married I command, yet not I but the Lord: A wife is not to depart from her husband. But even if she does depart, let her remain unmar-*

> *ried or be reconciled to her husband. And a husband is not to divorce his wife. But to the rest I, not the Lord, say: If any brother has a wife who does not believe, and she is willing to live with him, let him not divorce her. And a woman who has a husband, who does not believe, if he is willing to live with her, let her not divorce him.*

This suggests that Christians either stay single after divorce or go back to the one they married at first; they must wait until the erstwhile spouse dies before they can remarry. The cultural shift in the worldview of monogamy from one person, until death do us part, to one spouse at a time seems to have seeped into Christian culture. We simply should not cherry-pick spouses like the rest of the world because that is not what marriage is about. We marry primarily to manifest the image of God as I have explained all through this book. Many may not know this, but when man and woman come together in matrimony, a revelation of God takes place.

"*So God created man in His own image; in the image of God He created him; male and female He created them*" (Genesis 1:27).

The other reason we marry is to raise godly children with whom to populate God's earth. All the reasons we think we get married for are simply a mirage as many come to find out later. It is one of God's many open secrets—we marry for Him.

Aside from the psychological and financial problems that accompany marrying another person while the first spouse is still living, there are overlooked spiritual implications.

Know the Mission of Your Marriage

A marriage without a mission is no marriage at all. We have said that God chose marriage generically for populating the earth with godly people. Malachi 2:15 provides ample evidence of this. However, God has a specific mission for every marriage, which He reveals in prayer. Adam and Eve had a mission. Genesis 1:28 states, "*Then God blessed them, and God said to them, 'Be fruitful and multi-*

ply; fill the earth and subdue it; have dominion over the fish of the sea, over the birds of the air, and over every living thing that moves on the earth."

Marrying people without the direction or approval of the Holy Spirit will lead to a very different life from the one God planned for you and the person He intended for you to marry. This means that Christians ought to seek the Lord about their life's mission ahead of marriage and then seek the Lord about who best to travel with on their journey of life.

> *But as it is written: "Eye has not seen, nor ear heard, nor have entered into the heart of man the things, which God has prepared for those who love Him." But God has revealed them to us through His Spirit. For the Spirit searches all things, yes, the deep things of God. For what man knows the things of a man except the spirit of the man which is in him? Even so, no one knows the things of God except the Spirit of God. Now we have received, not the spirit of the world, but the Spirit who is from God, that we might know the things that have been freely given to us by God.* (1 Corinthians 2:9–12)

In 2001, as I was becoming increasingly aware of the ministry of the Holy Spirit, I began to inquire about my life's mission, who I would marry, and God's overall purpose for my life. Back then, I would spend time talking with the Lord on a variety of subjects that would concern any young Christian at that time. What I found was that persisting in prayer and learning the art of listening to God were of immense benefit; God's Spirit would reveal things as minute as the unexpected visit of a friend and as significant as the mission of my own life. He still does so today, and while I go into details in some of my other books, the impact of revelation knowledge cannot be overemphasized.

Let God's Spirit show you His mission for your life and, by extension, your marriage long before you meet the one. Whether you are married or single, knowing your life's mission first bears profound importance because, with it, you can get clarity as to your marriage's mission.

God Designed Marriage for the Finish Line

In his widely acclaimed book *the Dip,* marketing guru Seth Godin introduced a concept of the same name as the secret to attaining number one status in every human endeavor. The dip simply means persevering through the right things long enough while quitting the things you are not suited for to reach world number one status. Since God designed marriage and He designed it to be till death and not to end in divorce, it means that getting to the finish line will require reliance on Him. You will have to persevere to attain the point of inosculation, change the state of your marriage, and achieve the mutuality of everything with your spouse until your marriage aligns with how God defines it. *We* will have to supplant words like *I*, *me*, and *you* in both thought and speech if you and your spouse are to reach the finish line.

It does not matter that you chose your spouse for whatever reason you did. The facts are these: God joined you both together and no one, including yourselves, have His permission to take your marriage apart. The sliver of chance you have to make your marriage work is accepting the oneness that God established when you came together with your spouse as husband and wife.

Love and Attachment Are Not the Same

Many marriages are not really marriages as much as they are cohabiting arrangements. There is very little knowledge as to the interplay of love and attachment such that one is misconstrued for the other. Some marriages abound in love but are deficient in attachment. We call them partnerships. Others have strong attachment and weak love. These are codependent marriages. The interplay between the two is exactly like the Taoist yin and yang. Love gives, while attachment takes. God designed marriage to cater to both love and attachment, even though they are not the same. However, love is nothing without the feeling of attachment and vice versa.

When I was finishing the first draft of this manuscript, it had been four years since I first learned the concept, which I've tried, to the best of my God-given knowledge, to communicate in this book. My wife and I have been able to steer our marriage from the brink of divorce into a more perfect union despite the challenges common to life.

"You and I" is dismembering, while "we" is encompassing, embracing, and empowering.

About the Author

Patrick Igbinijesu is a commentator on Christian issues, specializing in the application of the message of the Bible to daily living. His mission is to build up a people through the impartation of God's Word so they can understand the reality of Jesus more intimately.

In this book, he addresses the issues of marriage, divorce, and parenting from a refreshing biblical standpoint while giving cognizance to the popular nuances surrounding these issues.

Although born in Nigeria, he recently moved to Canada where he lives with his wife and two children.